PLAYS BY WOMEN
VOLUME SEVEN

Thatcher's Women *by Kay Adshead*, Adult Child/Dead Child *by Claire Dowie*, Stamping, Shouting and Singing Home *by Lisa Evans*, Night *by Marie Laberge*, Effie's Burning *by Valerie Windsor*.

This is the seventh volume in Methuen's series of anthologies demonstrating the wide range of style and subject matter tackled by women playwrights. Kay Adshead's *Thatcher's Women* takes a look at the way in which three northern women, spurred on by poverty, desperation and a contemporary spirit of 'enterprise', get on their bikes to London to go into business – as prostitutes. Claire Dowie's *Adult Child/Dead Child* uses a skilful mixture of monologue and poetry to take us on a relentless and acutely painful journey through the life and perceptions of an abused and disturbed child. Inspired by the life of Sojourner Truth, the abolitionist and early feminist, Lisa Evan's *Stamping, Shouting and Singing Home* tells the story of her fictional great-great-granddaughter's transformation from child to adult activist in the southern states of America. In *Night* by French-Canadian playwright Marie Laberge, a silent woman and her garrulous father wait out the dark hours in a motel room where a fatal struggle for power is played out between them. In Valerie Windsor's *Effie's Burning*, a young doctor finds, in the inarticulate but powerful rage of an elderly woman mental patient, the key to her own suppressed anger and courage.

Each play has an afterword by its author and the volume itself opens with an introduction by the editor, Mary Remnant.

PLAYS BY WOMEN

Volume Seven

THATCHER'S WOMEN
by
Kay Adshead

ADULT CHILD/DEAD CHILD
by
Claire Dowie

STAMPING, SHOUTING AND SINGING HOME
by
Lisa Evans

NIGHT
by
Marie Laberge
translated by
Rina Fraticelli

EFFIE'S BURNING
by
Valerie Windsor

Edited and introduced by
Mary Remnant

A Methuen Paperback

A METHUEN NEW THEATRESCRIPT

This volume first published in Great Britain as a Methuen paperback original in 1988 by Methuen London Ltd., Michelin House, 81 Fulham Road, London SW3 6RB and in the United States of America by Methuen Inc., 29 West 35th Street, New York, NY 10001

British Library Cataloguing in Publication Data

Plays by women – (Methuen's new theatre
  scripts).
  Vol. 7 edited and introduced by Mary
  Remnant
  1. Drama in English, Women writers, 1945–
  Anthologies
  I. Remnant, Mary
  822'.914'0809287

ISBN 0-413-17490-5

Printed and bound in Great Britain by
Richard Clay Ltd, Bungay, Suffolk

CONTENTS

INTRODUCTION

This is the seventh volume in Methuen's series of anthologies of plays by women playwrights. The anthologies are published more or less annually and every year the same questions crop up again and again: Do we still need to 'ghettoise' women's work in this way? Do we still need to give women a special space in the world of published playscripts? Aren't enough women getting their work staged, and therefore having their scripts published individually, along with the men? The idea seems to have taken hold (among almost everyone except women playwrights and directors) that the volume of women's work making it onto our subsidised stages has increased dramatically. However, the hard facts expose this myth. The 1987 survey 'What Share of the Cake? The Employment of Women in the English Theatre'* makes depressing reading. With regard to Arts Council funding:

> The research shows that for every level of appointment that might be expected to have a significant impact on theatre policy, where women hold such posts, they are disadvantaged financially, and therefore artistically, compared with men in the same posts. In most posts, women are more likely than men with the same job title to be working with small theatre companies with low levels of funding, with small-scale touring companies without a permanent building base, or in theatres with small auditoria, and they are less likely than men to obtain employment outside London. (p.3)

The survey goes on to say that, if the one woman recently appointed as one of the five artistic directors of the National Theatre is excluded, women account for only 15 per cent of building-based artistic directors controlling only 5 per cent of building-based funding, and 34 per cent of all artistic directors, controlling only 8 per cent of total funding. This appalling state of affairs is inevitably reflected in the type and number of women's plays achieving production. In the twelve months preceding Caroline Gardiner's research, only 11 per cent of works performed were original works by women playwrights, the same as the figure found in an earlier study, 'The Status of Women in the British Theatre 1982–1983'.† And both figures include Agatha Christie! Not much has changed in the intervening period, it would seem.

Yet more women than ever are writing plays. They are involving themselves in workshops (for example, The Women's Playhouse Trust's current challenging series, 'Leaving the Margin', and, again in London, the Albany Empire's splendid 'Second Wave' activities), in writing and reading groups and, undoubtedly, are writing away in isolation too, with very little hope of seeing their work staged unless they have the time, energy and expertise to raise funds – scarce at the best of times and particularly unforthcoming to lesbian playwrights, partly as a result of the Government's anti-homosexual legislation – to mount their own shoe-string productions.

Where are the fruits of all this intense activity? Meagre they may be in terms of the volume of women's plays reaching our stages. Nevertheless, there can be no doubt that women playwrights are making an important and, it could be argued, currently the most exciting contribution to British theatre, as a look at some of the productions of the last fifteen months, since Volume Six of *Plays by Women* went to press, will show.

*'What Share of the Cake? The Employment of Women in the English Theatre' by Caroline Gardiner (commissioned and published by The Women's Playhouse Trust, London, 1987)

†'The Status of Women in the British Theatre 1982–1983' (Conference of Women Theatre Directors and Administrators, London, 1984); this study did not indicate whether or not works other than original works were included in the analysis.

In 1988 alone we have seen three plays by new writer Lucy Gannon – literally a 'kitchen table' writer, discovered when her play *Keeping Tom Nice* (currently showing in the RSC season at the Almeida), about the effects on a family of caring for a mentally disabled son and brother, won the Richard Burton Award. Earlier in the year, *Raping the Gold*, in which she treats the familiar theme of long-term unemployment with passion and anger, received rave reviews when staged at the Bush, while her short, 40-minute play *Janet and John*, a painful tragedy of ageing coupledom, was produced by the RSC at the Barbican. Other new writers include Soraya Jinton, whose *Lalita's Way*, an engaging and articulate response to changing cultural values in the form of a young Asian woman's attempts to avoid an arranged marriage, was seen as part of the Royal Court's Young Writers Festival, as was Hannah Vincent's *The Burrow*, a merciless satire-cum-horror-tale of suburbia based on a Kafka short story. April de Angelis followed her *Breathless* Second Wave debut with a Resisters production of *Women in Law*, an off-beat thriller, while Yana Stajno's first play, *Salt River*, explored the complexities of apartheid through the dynamics of the relationships between four women, one white Jewish liberal, two Cape Coloured and one black, in a production by the Pascal Theatre Company. Another first was Clean Break's production of Rena Owen's *Te Awa I Tahutu (The River That Ran Away)*, a testament to the devastating psychological cost of the white man's destruction of tribal cultures, a compulsively confessional autobiographical account by a mixed-blood Maori and herion-user. The Women's Theatre Group continued its excellent work with *Lear's Daughters*, Elaine Feinstein's first stage play, devised with the company, which explored the theme of women and power by asking how Regan, Goneril and Cordelia got to be the way they were, and what happened to their mother; and followed it up with Winsome Pinnock's *Picture Palace*, a look at the celluloid fantasies which inform all our lives.

Other women's companies doing good work are Charabanc, Spare Tyre, Hard Labour, Trouble and Strife and Theatre of Black Women. Charabanc's *Somewhere Over the Balcony* by Marie Jones, is a fast-moving running commentary with songs, about three women living in Belfast's Divis Flats, which applies a surreal humour to the grimness of their lives, producing a desperate and desperately funny celebration of the human spirit. Spare Tyre's *Head Over Heels*, a rueful comment on women's magazines, debunks the idea that mindless romanticism and women's genuine interest in feelings are the same thing, and, in passing, celebrates lesbianism while mourning the oppression of lesbians. *Prison Baby* by Cheryl Moskowitz and Hard Labour makes a powerful connection between the sexual subordination of women in society and the state's system of punishment, through the image of the double confinement of a woman both pregnant and in prison. Also set in a prison, in Armagh gaol in September 1980 during the women's 'no wash' protest, Trouble and Strife's *Now And At the Hour of Our Death*, by Sonja Lyndon and the company, explores the dialectic between violent action and peaceful resistance, as four women, part of the campaign to achieve the status of political prisoners, draw on enormous resources of courage, discipline and fury to survive deprivation and humiliation. In Ruth Harris's *The Cripple*, Theatre of Black Women aimed to destroy myths about people with disabilities, with a one-woman monologue of strength, stamina and determination. What we are seeing in all these shows is a theatre of survival and struggle, against misogyny, against imperialism of all kinds, against the prejudices which are so much a part of the fabric of our society. It is not a struggle engaged in with grim grit-your-teeth- and-wait-till-it-goes-away stoicism but rather with purposeful anger, energy and, above all, humour. And here I must mention a visiting company, the South African Vusisizwe Players, whose funny and moving *You Strike the Woman You Strike the Rock*, set in a township on the outskirts of Cape Town, shows how women disempowered by a cruel system can draw strength and courage from each other.

Courage can be found in seemingly unlikely ways, as Frances McNeil's unusual *Jehad*, about a young single mother who finds purpose and salvation by embracing Islam, testifies; while Penny O'Connor's *Dig Volley Spike*, about a women's volley-ball team, looks at the contradictions of ambition, competitiveness and women's conditioning to fail. *Blood, Sweat and Fears* by Marie Oshodi, an absorbing play about sickle cell anaemia, which affects around 10 per cent of Britain's black community, treats the problems surrounding this still relatively ignored illness with compassion, and is also extremely funny. Annie Griffin's *Almost Persuaded*, a complex and witty piece of theatre, takes its title from the Tammy Wynette song and uses Country & Western music and the lives of its stars and fans to examine the image of women, highlighting the role-playing into which women are so often forced; and illusion and reality also come into conflict in Jane Beeson's *The Cradle Will Rock*, a sad play about the high expectations and low esteem surrounding motherhood. Motherhood looms large again in Julia Kearsley's *Under the Web*, an unsentimental study in social labelling and rigid gender roles, as a woman deals with the multiple demands of single parenthood, caring for her own infirm mother, and trying to have a life of her own as well. Motherhood again features, in an Irish play, Nell McCafferty's *The Worm in the Heart* ('Romance is the worm in the heart of feminism,'). Guilt-laden, mystical assertions about motherhood are the worm in the heart of this play, but nevertheless it works as a shocking reminder of what life is like for women just over the water, where there is no abortion, no divorce and very little room for manoeuvre. A notable achievement is Sheila Yeger's *Self Portrait*, an exciting, intriguing and satisfying biography of Gwen John, exploring complex issues such as women's roles and the artist as obsessive, raising it above the usual level of stage biographies. And at the 1987 Edinburgh Festival Liz Lochhead's *Mary Queen of Scots Got Her Head Chopped Off* provided a poetic, witty and sardonic alternative to the grandeur of Schiller's *Mary Stuart*, another festival production. Lochhead's play is full of dramatic and comic invention, music and dance, and sharp dialogue, another biography that blasts myths in order to say something of relevance to contemporary womanhood. Also seen at Edinburgh, a welcome and very powerful play was Anna Reading's *Kiss Punch Goodnight*. Explicit, harrowing and shocking, the play pulls no punches in its premise that power and not love or sexual desire underlies child sexual abuse.

   The Memorial Gardens by lesbian playwrights Maro Green and Caroline Griffin is a funny, tender and radical play, with its story of two women, friends in the sixties, lovers considering having a child in the eighties, looking at the abuse of power and challenging received ideas of family, religion and love. For pure fun, Cheryl Moch's lesbian panto, *Cinderella the Real True Story*, complete with Princess Charming and ugly brothers, inverted the traditional story to encompass all the fables of fairy tale. And Red Rag's *The Infamous Life and Crimes of Nell Undermine* was a frantic, funny and fast-moving flight of fancy, giving a potted herstory of the female character as outsider.

   There were also some revivals worth noting. Beth Henley's Pulitzer prize-winning *Crimes of the Heart* caught the tone and texture of small-town life and the wounding hurts of family in a play filled with warmth and humanity. *Will You Still Need Me?* by Ena Lamont Stewart, best known for 7:84's 1983 revival of *Men Should Weep*, was given its British première. Slight and limited in scope, this trilogy of beautifully observed studies of the hurts, betrayals and loneliness suffered by women nevertheless achieved unfailing emotional truth. Foco Novo's elegant and elliptical production of Marguerite Duras' *Savannah Bay*, an exquisitely poetic piece about a girl who gives birth and dies in Savannah Bay, did justice to the haunting, musical quality of Duras' prose, in its attempt to recover the past through key images. John Barton's production of Aphra Behn's *The Rover*, considerably cut and reworked, didn't, however, manage to blunt her main point that men invent moral laws for their own convenience and that women are fully entitled to sexual freedom; while Mary Wortley Montagu's *Simplicity*, substantially based on Marivaux's *Game of Love and Chance*, is a play of social and emotional manners, observed in sequences of cool satire, the prologue and epilogue of letters written by Montagu, principally to her husband, giving an added, bitter dimension.

   This is, of necessity, a very selective survey, but gives, I hope, a flavour of the rich diversity and scope of women's writing for the theatre at the present time.

The five plays which comprise this volume couldn't be more different from each other: different in style and content; different, no doubt, in the impulses from which they spring. Yet each is a satisfying whole, making its own contribution to the growing reservoir of women's recorded experience.

Thatcher's Women by Kay Adshead may, at first glance, seem the most conventional: a naturalistic, deeply depressing comment on contemporary hardship and survival. But this story of three northern women, forced to desperate lengths by the Thatcher Government's economic policies, is also strangely uplifting for, as the play progresses, naturalism slides off into surreal imagery, adding a poetic dimension to an ironic tale of 'free enterprise'. I recall, at the time the play was staged, one critic's comment that its main flaw was that the women did not stop to consider their decision to pack their bags and make off for two weeks 'on the game' in London. Where was the moral dilemma, he asked. How could ordinary, decent women opt for prostitution without a second thought? The sort of comment one might expect from a white, middle-class, male theatre critic. First comes unemployment, poverty – and we're not talking about tightening our belts in cheaper restaurants or cancelling *The Economist*; we're talking about having the electric cut off, not knowing where the next meal is coming from, being beaten by a despairing husband. First comes poverty, then desperation – the moral dilemma comes later. The desperate have nothing to lose, and the play's image of Marje, the 'ordinary, decent' woman turned prostitute, sharpening her teeth on dispossession, along with the urban foxes, is one which will stay with me for a long time.

Despite Claire Dowie's own claim that the protagonist of *Adult Child/Dead Child* is androgynous, it never occurred to me, seeing and reading the play, that she wasn't female, if only because it's hard to imagine a family where a son is spurned and a daughter can do no wrong. Dowie's dark poetic monologue is an acutely painful confession of lovelessness, loneliness and the loss of self, made all the more poignant by the character's insistence that s/he 'was never what you'd call an abused child': cruelly disciplined, reared on a merciless 'eye for eye, tooth for tooth' philosophy, locked in broom cupboards and, above all, totally unloved, but not 'abused'. The 'adult child/dead child' of this play walks the fine line – a tightrope – between the perversion of adult power over children, and abuse. It's almost impossible to convey the harrowing intensity of Dowie's work – read it.

Lisa Evans's *Stamping, Shouting and Singing Home* is, as its title suggests, a celebration; not the loss of self but a search for and discovery of identity, as Lizzie Walker, fictional great-great-granddaughter of abolitionist and early feminist, Sojourner Truth, is transformed from child to adult activist in the southern states of America. Inspired by a rich tradition of verbal herstory and by her own sister's politicisation and death through resistance, Lizzie sloughs off the dead weight of Hollywood stereotypes, big white lies, and oppression both as a black and as a woman, and emerges fearless, joyful and full of resolve.

When I first read *Night* (*L'Homme gris*) by French-Canadian playwright Marie Laberge in a translation by Rina Fraticelli – it struck me as one of the most powerful evocations I've ever come across of a man trying to swallow a woman whole. And, indeed, food is an important metaphor in the play. Roland eats greedily while Christine can hardly get anything down, and vomits up what she does. Roland also talks – endlessly – munching away at Christine with his words, while she remains largely silent except for a few stammered words and exclamations. And he devours her with his eyes – eyes which look, eyes which dissect, but eyes which do not see Christine, until she finally has to cut them out of him. Don't read this one on a full stomach!

Valerie Windsor's *Effie's Burning* is a wonderful play – a small and shining gem. When Dr Ruth Kovacs is commanded by her pompous consultant to see to the burns of elderly mental patient Effie, she begins to uncover a story of injustice, bigotry and callousness which stuns her into incredulity and then catapults her into resolution. Raped at eleven, pregnant, institutionalised and branded as a 'moral defective' at twelve, kept in a mental asylum until well into her sixties, and then shoved out into the 'community', Effie may be slow and inarticulate, but she has her own way of expressing her towering rage. At the heart of the play is the metaphor of spontaneous combustion, and it is the key to Dr Kovacs' own suppressed anger and courage. Dr Kovacs' fear that 'if I once let one half of what's in here out, then the ceilings would crack, the floors would open, the roofs fly off slate by slate into the air, girders buckle, pavements open up, forests rip apart and swirl into the clouds, the seas boil, the skies grow black' will be grippingly familiar to any woman who has mutilated herself with self-control in the face of the million large and small humiliations and cruelties of misogyny. Dr Kovacs comes to recognise the constructive as well as the destructive power of her anger. I hope this play is produced again and again.

So here they are, five plays – a very small drop in the ocean of women's theatre writing. I hope they make you greedy for more.

THATCHER'S WOMEN

Kay Adshead

Characters

The play needs 6 actors: 4 women and 2 men (1 young man, 1 middle aged).

Marje, *late 30s*
Norah, *mid-30s*
Lynda, *17*

The other parts double as follows:

Young woman	JESS/CARESS
Young man	ALAN/COLIN/ALISTAIR/JOHNNY/POLICEMAN/ MAN IN PENTHOUSE
Middle-aged man	MAN AT TEA STAND/DEL/STAN/MAN ON COMMON/ DESMOND

The play can be performed on a simple multifunctional set, possibly with different levels – leaving the sound tape to establish the whereabouts where possible – but nothing should be mimed and the first scene should approximate real conditions.

The play is set in Manchester and London. The action takes place between August and December 1985.

Thatcher's Women was first produced by Paines Plough at the Tricycle Theatre, London, on 12 March 1987 with the following cast:

MARJE	Marjorie Yates
NORAH	Rachel Davies
LYNDA	Debra Gillet
ALAN, JOHNNY, POLICEMAN, *etc.*	Jonathan Stratt
DEL, ALISTAIR, STAN, *etc.*	Robin Soans
JESS, CARESS	Amanda Symonds

Directed by Pip Broughton
Designed by Ellen Cairns
Lighting Designer Jim Simmons
Sound by Colin Brown
Assistant Director Debbie Seymour
Stage Manager Rosie Cullen
Production Manager Chris Corner
Technical Stage Manager Claire Le May
Set built by Nick Redgrave
Production Photographs Sarah Ainslie
Poster Design Ian Laynn
Music Charles Lineham, Dennis Verdon-Martinez

A finishing-room in a tinned-meat-pudding factory in the north

Sound tape: deafening factory noise. Lights snap up. The bottom end of a finishing-line. Three women bend over large metal baskets full of tins. Two face each other, the line in between. The third is on her own, opposite an empty basket. They work with astonishing speed and dexterity 'picking' the tins, slotting them on the line, bending further down as the baskets empty.

The factory noise is taken down, though never stops, and the women pitch their voices to be heard over it.

The tins roll upstage and out of sight.

NORAH: . . . so then she told them she'd been employed as a factory worker, not a lavatory cleaner.

LYNDA: That's quite right.

NORAH: What do you mean? All she's got to do is put a cloth over the seat, fluff up the bog roll . . . yank the chain a few times, that's all I do –

MARJE: She's rather particular, you know Dolly.

NORAH: Then a nice quiet fag till hooter.

MARJE: P'raps she was worried about germs.

NORAH (*seriously*): Why, she doesn't have to suck lavatory brush, does she?

LYNDA (*shudders*): Ugh!

NORAH: No – if you ask me, that puffy husband put her up to it.

MARJE: Ron isn't puffy, he's . . . artistic.

NORAH: What! Just cos he shops in Safeways in flipflops.

MARJE: He's done some lovely pictures for Dolly's hall, remember that one of the horse's head she showed us.

NORAH: Horse's head! Is that what it was? Straight up. I thought it was a coal scuttle.

They laugh.

No, he's always had fancy ideas has Ron. Look what he's done to that house – Dolly was frightened to put milk bottles out one time . . . case they got pebble-dashed.

More laughter. A young man in a starched white coat and straw trilby, carrying a clipboard sweeps past.

ALAN: Morning ladies . . . (*Softly:*) Morning Norah. (*He scratches his nose.*)

ALL: Morning Alan.

NORAH *slowly straightens herself from the basket and gazes after him . . . pause.*

NORAH (*softly*): I wish they'd find a way of putting that in a tin.

LYNDA: I don't know what you see in him, I think he's wet. I hate the way he always scratches his nose when he's embarrassed.

NORAH: Do you? I love that. Body language that is, you know. It's sort of like saying, I want to gaze into your limpid green eyes, Norah, but I daren't, I'm shy – I'm afraid.

LYNDA: Our dog always scratches is nose when he wants to go out.

NORAH (*ignoring this, staring after him*): There's something about a man in a white coat, really turns me on . . . hospital doctors . . . dentists . . . psychiatrists.

LYNDA: Lollipop men.

NORAH *sneers at* LYNDA, *then continues to gaze off into the distance.* MARJE *looks over her shoulder.*

MARJE (*softly*): They're buzzing about this morning.

LYNDA: Shit! (*She stands up straight and takes off her glove, she shows them her hand.*) Look at that! It's taken me ages to grow them all the same length an' all.

NORAH (*seeing a huge 'diamond' ring on* LYNDA'*s finger*): Who gave you that?

LYNDA: Nobody, I bought it myself.

MARJE: Is it real?

LYNDA: Course not, if it was real I wouldn't be working here, would I.

MARJE: It's lovely anyway.

LYNDA (*getting ready to adjourn to the toilets with a nail file*): Well I'll tell you this much, they're going to have to get someone else in for Dolly, cos I'm not working a basket on my own and that's that.

She moves off.

MARJE: Where you going?

LYNDA: To suck a lavatory brush.

NORAH (*shudders*): Ugh!

MARJE: I'll say she's come on.

NORAH: Watch 'er! Olive's back.

The supervisor has taken her seat at the desk facing the finishing-lines. NORAH and MARJE work silently.

MARJE (*speaking as quietly as she can*): Norah, you couldn't see your way clear to lending me £5 . . . just till pay day?

NORAH: Bloody hell, it's only Monday.

MARJE: I know, only tomorrow's Terry's birthday, I've promised him a track suit and I'm £5 short.

NORAH: Can't you look for something cheaper?

MARJE: He's set his heart on that one.

NORAH: I suppose so – but you're going to have to tell Terry there's only one of you working now and they can't expect big expensive presents anymore. My kids have to make do.

MARJE: I'm trying to economise, I am really. Thanks Norah.

They work silently for a few minutes. The factory noise changes slightly; one of the other lines down the room has stopped.

NORAH: Eh up. Dopey Dillie's got her cuff caught in the plastic box again.

There is an increasing gaggle of voices from the far end of the finishing-room. One more line stops. LYNDA comes rushing towards them, breathless.

LYNDA: Eh, you know you were saying you were missing Dolly.

MARJE: Yes.

LYNDA: Well you're going to see more of her than you thought.

MARJE: What do you mean?

LYNDA: Notice has gone up. We're all laid off. Finishing-room closes in four weeks' time.

Their one remaining line stops suddenly.

Silence.

Lights snap to blackout.

Pritchard's executive toilet

Sound tape: in the distance a large party in full swing.
    Lights up. The light is dim. NORAH and ALAN are against a wall. Both are dishevelled. NORAH has just lit a cigarette. ALAN is putting himself to rights. They whisper.

ALAN: . . . Bellings, Harrison, all top management use this bog.

NORAH: I can see that, but then you know I wouldn't take you to any old toilet.

They laugh. NORAH hands him a cigarette.

ALAN: All that lager and stuff, best not push our luck eh?

NORAH: Push our luck?

ALAN: They'll all start missing us.

ALAN walks over to the mirror and starts combing his hair. NORAH watches.

So what'll you do now then, Norah?

NORAH: What do you mean?

ALAN: Now that you're a lady of leisure.

NORAH: I'll go back to medical college, get my degree, and become a brain surgeon.

ALAN finishes his ablutions and turns to NORAH.

ALAN: You look fabulous this afternoon. (*He pats her bum.*) I reckon you could be on the telly in that frock.

NORAH: On the telly?

ALAN: Yeah, you know, one of those game-show hostesses. (*He gets ready to leave.*)

NORAH: Oh I could do that. (*Taking his hand.*) Alan Banks – Come on Down!)

NORAH *holds* ALAN's *hand firmly on to her crutch.* ALAN *swallows. He looks nervously in the direction of the door. He tries to scratch his nose, but* NORAH *won't let his hand go. He scratches with the other hand.*

ALAN: They'll be pulling raffle soon – I reckon.

NORAH (*now well into it*): What would you rather have; a set of matching pot towels – or me?

ALAN (*he laughs, twiddling his lapel*): We've still got work to do this afternoon, when you lot have gone.

NORAH: Oh yeah. What's it say on your label?

ALAN: Quality control.

NORAH: What you get up to all day, I've always wondered?

ALAN: Well . . .

NORAH: Yes.

ALAN: We have to check that the number, that's the code on the label, corresponds to that in the outgoing book for that day.

NORAH: Yes.

ALAN: Check the tins aren't dented, discoloured, rusted.

NORAH: Yes.

ALAN: And the weight.

NORAH: I see. You're a fast worker Alan Banks, I'll say that.

ALAN *laughs nervously.*

NORAH: 'Quality Control', sounds like a posh cure for premature ejaculation to me.

ALAN: Sorry about that.

NORAH: Don't worry chucky egg, we've still got afters.

Blackout.

Marje's house

Sound tape: the faint ticking of a clock.
Lights up. DEL *is sitting on a chair.*
MARJE *enters.*

MARJE: I didn't tell you – we got a card from Billy . . . and the Todds.

DEL *says nothing.*

Debbie says can she put them on a string for us?

DEL (*softly*): Where you been?

MARJE (*sitting down*): Putting the kids to bed.

Silence.

(*Getting up:*) Let me get you a nice hot milky drink, it's cold in here.

DEL: I don't want a drink.

MARJE: It'll help you . . .

DEL (*quietly*): I'm not a bloody kid. If I say I don't want one, I don't.

Silence.

MARJE (*getting up*): I've got an evening paper.

DEL: Picked it out the rubbish bin?

MARJE: No, next door pass it on.

DEL: You what?

MARJE: He only gets it for the crossword.

DEL (*laughs*): Jesus, what'll they be passing on next – their bog roll?

MARJE *gets up.*

What now?

MARJE: I was going to move the light – it's shining in your eye . . .

DEL (*softly*): Leave it. Leave it . . . leave it.

Blackout.

Lynda's bedsit

Sound tape: the same slow ticking of a clock.
Lights up. LYNDA *is in a slip – she half sits, half kneels on a wooden chair facing out. She combs her hair, slowly, rhythmically . . . observing the static.*
Behind her COLIN *is in the final stages of getting dressed.*

COLIN (*very bright and breezy*): So who knows, this time next year I might be a regular army man . . . out in the tropics somewhere, Gibraltar maybe or . . . they really look after you these days you know . . . smart apartments, good food, cracking holidays, . . . it's a good life I reckon . . . well better than . . . what do you think?

Pause   LYNDA *says nothing.*
COLIN *is expected to leave.*

(*Softly:*) I er . . . saw Margaret last week, Lynda.

LYNDA: Oh yeah.

COLIN: She's working now, on one of these YOP things, it's a silk flower place – really enjoying it she is, they give her a wire and she wraps green ribbon round for the stem, when she's been there a couple of months they let her start on the p. . .

LYNDA (*laughs softly*): Do us a favour.

COLIN *swallows.*

COLIN: She'd like you to get in touch with her.

Pause.

(*Softly:*) I said she'd like you to –

LYNDA: I heard what you said.

Slight pause. LYNDA *still combing her hair.* COLIN *takes a few nervous paces.*

COLIN (*bright and breezy, trying again*): I went round to Jacko's. (*Chuckling:*) You should see his hair now, right down his back it is, I told him, I said . . .

LYNDA: Look Colin – I've got to be somewhere.

COLIN (*absolutely still*): Yes of course. (*Quietly:*) Go home Lynda, Eh? This is no life for you.

Pause.

You'd be better off at home with your family.

Pause.

(*He looks round:*) Just look around you for God's sake, it's filthy, it stinks . . . it's a rat hole and . . .

LYNDA (*turning on him, suddenly furious*): This place is temporary. All right?

She turns back and resumes combing her hair energetically.

Long pause. COLIN *sighs sheepishly. He gets out his wallet, he takes out*

three fivers and puts them in the accustomed place.

COLIN (*leaving*): You're a lovely girl, Lynda. I've always said that.

Blackout.

A street on a rainy night

Sound tape: heavy rain. The sound of cars skidding and swerving give way to women's slow footsteps . . . they stop.
Lights up. LYNDA *and* NORAH *under a railway bridge. Rain continues underneath the scene.*

LYNDA: It's not as bad as you think, Norah – I only really go with people I know, people I've sussed out, there's no risk at all if you're really careful.

NORAH (*fascinated*): Do your family know?

LYNDA: Of course they don't – nobody knows – so keep your big trap shut, all right.

A car speeds towards them. They are caught for a second in the light of the car's headlamps. LYNDA *turns to* NORAH.

I've had it with this dump, Norah. I've decided to pack it in here, go down to London for a bit.

NORAH: London! Lucky bleeder.

LYNDA: Why don't you come with me?

NORAH: Yer what?

LYNDA: Mickie's out of work, right?

NORAH: Yeah.

LYNDA: You're short of money.

NORAH: Naturally.

LYNDA: I'm right in thinking a couple of hundred pounds wouldn't come amiss.

NORAH: Go on.

LYNDA: Well, what if I told you you could earn two hundred pounds, and two hundred pounds on top if you packed a couple of bags, came down to London with me for a fortnight.

NORAH: Four hundred pounds . . . (*Pause.*) . . . oh no.

LYNDA: Why?

NORAH: Well, I'm not one am I?

LYNDA: I'm not one if it comes to that. Look I'm not asking you to leave everything, go on the game forever. I'm just saying why don't we go down London for a couple of weeks, earn a bit of easy money, before Christmas – that's all.

NORAH: Just like that.

LYNDA: Just like that.

NORAH: And meanwhile what do I tell my husband and three kids about this little trip – 'Am off to flog fanny in London, back soon, Mum.'

LYNDA: No – (*She gets a card out of her bag.*) You tell them you're going to work for Manpower Services on Gloucester Road. It's a legit agency that supplies casual labour to factories on the outskirts of London. I've a pal there who'll vouch for us. It pays well – £20, £30 a day for two weeks, and you're staying here. (*She gets out another card.*)

NORAH: You've got it all worked out, haven't you?

LYNDA: A girl I know keeps two rooms on, but only uses them from time to time. She'll let me borrow them, just till I get straight. Look, it'll cost you nothing. I'll even stand you the train fare.

NORAH: You're very eager aren't you?

LYNDA: I could do with the company, if you must know.

NORAH (*looking at the card, then handing it back*): Do you know, my sister-in-law went to London on a mini-weekend. She said walking from the train to the taxi she saw that bloke who used to be on 'Please Sir' . . . Lord Longford . . . and that Indian woman who does the cooking on TV AM . . . just walking from the train to the taxi.

LYNDA: Well?

NORAH: No, course not.

LYNDA: Why?

NORAH: I couldn't go through with it.

LYNDA: Course you could. Look – I know you, I wouldn't ask you if I

didn't think you could do it. I'd show you the ropes. It's dead easy, Norah, honest.

NORAH: No.

LYNDA: Don't tell me you think it's immoral. Coming from you I might just puke.

NORAH: You're a young girl, aren't you . . . you dress well and everything – I can see a bloke coughing up to have a go at you. . . . Look at me – I'm not exactly Raquel Welch am I, even in this light.

LYNDA (*laughing*): Look, some men don't like you to be too pretty – makes them feel uncomfortable. Loads of the plainer girls knock spots off my earnings.

NORAH: Well that's good to know.

LYNDA: Well?

Blackout.

Marje's house

Lights up. The room is in semi-darkness, lit only by several candles in saucers, some almost burnt through. Chairs are overturned, plates and cutlery from the table strewn over the floor. MARJE sits almost underneath. She's been beaten up. Her face is cut and bleeding.

NORAH (*off . . . rattling a doorknocker*): Is anyone home? (*Coming through the hall.*) You're asking for trouble aren't you – your front door's wide open (*She enters. Quietly to herself:*) What they having here? . . . A seance? (*She moves to the light switch, clicks it on . . . nothing . . . into the hall . . . clicks that switch . . , nothing. . . . Back into the room, her eyes get accustomed to the light. She spies MARJE under the table.*

NORAH (*going to her*): Jesus Christ! What the hell are you doing there? What's happened? Somebody's got in, haven't they? Where are the kids, Marje? Are the kids all right? (*She makes a move to the door.*)

MARJE (*heaving herself up to her elbows and then standing up*): Nobody's been in, Norah – the kids are all right.

NORAH (*looking at her*): Who's been at you?

MARJE: Nobody.

NORAH: Well, somebody's been at you. Even you couldn't beat yourself up. (*She looks round the room carefully for a moment.*) It's Del, isn't it? I don't believe it. I don't believe what I'm seeing.

MARJE: Get me a cup of water, will you?

Pause. NORAH examines MARJE's face.

NORAH: I'd best get you something for that eye while I'm at it.

She moves into the kitchen, automatically flicks the light switch.

What's happened to your lights?

She pops her head back round the door.

What's happened to your lights?

MARJE: Electricity's been cut off.

NORAH: What!

MARJE: This afternoon.

NORAH: Why?

MARJE: Why do you think? I haven't paid the bill.

NORAH: They can't do that. Not when there's children. They have to give you notice.

MARJE: I've had the notice, Norah. I just haven't had the money.

NORAH leans on the table.

NORAH: You stupid cow! How many times have I told you to work out your money, put a bit away each week?

MARJE: I have been putting money away, Norah, honestly I have.

NORAH: So?

MARJE: I've been taking it out again.

NORAH: Why?

MARJE: The kids have needed that much – pumps for Terry one week, tights for Debbie the next.

NORAH: Those bleeding kids. Where are they now?

MARJE: Del's taken them to his mother's. It's not safe for them here, he says. He's right, it's not.

NORAH: And is he coming back?

MARJE (*very quietly*): I don't know.

NORAH: Well, he better bleeding had. I don't see why you should face this singlehanded. He's your husband, isn't he? He's got to do something besides trying to thump sense into you.

MARJE (*very quietly*): He didn't mean it, Norah. Today was the last straw with him – he lost his temper and he lashed out, but he'll be sorry now, I'm sure of that.

Pause. NORAH and MARJE sit for some time in the candlelight.

It's funny you know, but it was all right when he was first laid off, he was here for the kids coming home, that was a help to me. Course, the money was tight (*Pause.*) Then I got laid off. He used to go for these long walks, have I told you, sometimes a whole day would go by and I wouldn't see him. He'd come in worn out, almost as if he'd done a day's work. . . .

Yesterday morning I popped out to the shops, just for a loaf and a pint of milk. There'd been the first real frost of the winter. All the streets looked sparkly and sprinkled with sugar.

. . . Then I saw Terry and Debbie racing up the street – 'Come quick Mum, Dad's making funny noises' – 'Get the doctor,' I said, 'run and get the doctor'.

The door was wide open, like tonight, and at the front gate I could hear him, hear the funny noises. It wasn't a seizure or a heart attack or anything – he was sobbing, that's all. Del was sobbing, nothing to worry about after all. That's all the funny noises were.

Pause. NORAH listens.

We've had £10 to last us nine days. That's if Debbie and Terry walk to school. I'll meet them in the afternoon cos it's dark now by four, and I worry about them coming down that hill on their own. . . .

Course, Christmas coming doesn't help. That doesn't help anything.

Silence. They both sit quite still, thinking.

NORAH: I saw Lynda tonight, Marje. She put something to me.

NORAH *and* MARJE *stay still but not frozen within the scene. Lights stay as they are.*

LYNDA *walks into the scene. She stands centre-stage, facing the audience.*

LYNDA (*briskly*): Rule 1: Never do it without a rubber. If he's got a 'Johnny' on you've less chance of picking something up.

Rule 2: If you do get something – I've had NSU and I get cystitis all the time – have it checked right away at the nearest clap clinic. They'll always treat your case in total confidence.

Rule 3: If they do turn nasty – and they do – never show you're frightened. Stand your ground, raise your voice. If they think they're going to be part of a scene they'll lose their nerve and scarper.

Rule 4: Try and get all the money off him at the start. This way if he's huffing and puffing and getting nowhere you can always tell him time's up and he's had his chips.

Rule 5: Set a time limit – twenty minutes at the most, and never go over it unless they're paying extra, obviously.

Rule 6: Avoid picking up in places known to the police. I work the bowling alley, local library, even the local Conservative Club. I do less business but although I've had a couple of warnings I've never been busted.

Rule 7: Never drink on the job. Keep your wits about you. If there's something about him you don't like, steer clear. Life's too short, why take risks?

Rule 8: If you have to go with somebody you haven't sussed out, never take him back – try and do it somewhere where there's people not too far away and there's plenty of light. Similarly never get into a car.

NORAH (*whispers to* MARJE): Lynda reckons she clears £360 a week.

LYNDA: Rule 9: I'll only do straight sex or hand jobs. I've never done oral or Greek, but I suppose it's up to you to decide what you'll do.

NORAH: She reckons it'll be £500 down there.

LYNDA: Rule 10: Don't get too greedy. More than three or four a night and your judgement starts going. Know when to call it a night.

MARJE: I could get myself straight with that, wipe the slate clean . . . be able to buy kids' Christmas presents, everything.

NORAH: Do you think Del'll swallow it?

MARJE: He will if I tell him it's all through Pritchard's. I'll say Olive rang – it's only two weeks, he can cope for that long.

NORAH: Oh yeah, it's only a fortnight. I mean it's not like we're really going on the game – more of a trip out . . .

Gradually, the sounds of a busy railway station. Announcements on a loud speaker.

. . . a bit of a giggle eh? . . . girls together . . . it'll be like we're sixteen all over again Marje – best frocks, high heels, 15 denier – a bit of tutti – I tell you, the big smoke won't know what's hit it.

. . . I've never been to London – they say it's lovely at Christmas, all the shops, and the fairy lights. I'll get to see a few sights p'raps. . . . Buckingham Palace, Trafalgar Square. . . .

Marje's journey to King's Cross

Sound tape: in the background a moving train.

Lights up. NORAH *and* LYNDA *are now seated.* MARJE, *centre-stage.*

MARJE: Sunday afternoons . . . George Formby on the telly. The long bus ride to me grandma's house. She'd lived in that house since she was married, before that she'd lived in the same house two streets away . . . all the houses in all the streets, two-ups, two-downs, streets and streets, built for the mill, for me grandma was a mill hand.

At six o'clock, the mill siren would stop the dreams in the mill houses and send hundreds on the long misty trudge up Pigalle Hill.

When the mill closed down my grandma went to work at the shirt factory on the buttonholing machine. In the war she worked in the munitions factory making bombs. then went back to the buttonholing, then they put her on collar and cuffs – then on shirt tails – round hemming.

Two-ups, two-downs – white stone steps. Parlour with the pot shepherd boy, hands in his pockets, whistling – the back room where my grandma sat, the scullery, backyard, outside lav, yard door, opening on to the entry. . . . On the other side of the entry was a brick wall, 20 – 30 – 40 feet, on the top, sharpened steel rods, and barbed wire – for the houses backed on to Belle Vue.

The train picks up speed.

At the front, on the road, there was a green arch with blue and yellow letters: 'Welcome to Belle Vue Zoo'. There was a kiddies' playground with plaster giraffes and monkeys and hippos, and concrete tubs full of geraniums, and on bank holidays a man dressed up as a clown handing out balloons.

From the house there was just the great brick wall.

On the other side of the wall was the lion house, the tiger house, the elephant house.

Sitting in the back room with my granma, watching George Formby on the telly, we would hear the low roars and bellows, the pounding and threshing of wild creatures.

One Sunday afternoon, we heard a great scream over our heads, over all the streets and houses. One of the lions – or tigers – or leopards – had looked at the brick wall and the sharpened steel rods and the barbed wire – and remembered.

The great screech of brakes as the train enters a station.

Blackout.

A room in a King's Cross guest house

Lights up.

LYNDA *is looking at her face in a handbag mirror.* NORAH *and* MARJE *are around her trying to help.* JESS *sits on one of the beds smoking.*

A small TV is on loud.

NORAH: She'll need ice on that.

MARJE: I don't think there is any, is there?

LYNDA: If she'd have told me to go I would have done.

MARJE: Cold water'll do. I'll soak this.

MARJE *takes the towel and moves in to the next room.*

LYNDA: Nobody told me it was her flaming pitch.

NORAH: There's nothing broken anyway.

LYNDA: One minute I was standing there minding my own business, next minute the incredible hulk's on top of me.

NORAH: You'll have a fat lip, mind.

LYNDA: Vicious cow. I could have the law on her.

JESS *smirks.*

If I'm marked that's it – I might as well go home now and I've forked out £80 on this place already.

She storms out as MARJE *re-enters, and snatches the towel.*

The 9 o'clock news is on TV. MARJE *turns it off.*

An uneasy silence.

NORAH: Thanks for bringing her back, Mrs . . .

JESS: Jess.

NORAH: Thanks.

JESS: You her mother?

NORAH: No, I'm not her bleeding mother.

JESS *laughs.*

MARJE: We're friends.

JESS: Oh yeah.

NORAH: Yes.

Pause.

JESS: Where you from?

MARJE: Manchester.

JESS: Part-timers, eh?

MARJE: Sorry?

JESS: How long you here for?

MARJE: Two weeks.

JESS (*laughs*): S'truth.

Slight pause.

Don't get me wrong but I'd take tonight as a warning if I was you.

NORAH: A warning?

JESS: Regular girls round here had enough with you lot last year.

NORAH: Us lot?

JESS: Coming down, picking up the Christmas trade, taking over girls' pitches, underselling. How much the little girl charge out there tonight?

NORAH: Ten woodbines?

JESS: Doing it without rubbers. I tell you, regular girls are sick of it. She got off very lightly. Next time she could find herself carved, never mind clobbered.

Silence.

NORAH: Jesus. . . . Excuse me . . . I er, think I'll take a look at her.

She exits.

JESS (*laughs*): Seen that type before. Have a taste for it, so they think they can make money with it. She'll be on the train back home by the end of the week.

Pause. JESS *is looking at* MARJE.

Little girl could make out, but not round here. . . . Paddington'd be better for her, or up West. Got any contacts?

MARJE: Contacts?

JESS: Addresses of people who'll put business your way.

MARJE: No.

JESS: What about Meryl?

MARJE: Meryl?

JESS: She uses these rooms, don't she?

MARJE: I don't know.

JESS: Friend of Lynda's is she?

MARJE: I don't know.

JESS: Expect so. Looks her type . . . she struck lucky with a punter . . . taken her abroad, has he?

MARJE: I don't know.

JESS: You don't know much, do you?

MARJE (*laughs*): No.

JESS: Still, nice and comfy here. (*She begins to walk around the room.*)

Trouble at home then?

MARJE: Sort of.

JESS: There would be wouldn't there. . . . You married?

MARJE (*softly*): Yes.

JESS: Your old man know you're here?

MARJE: No.

JESS: Where he think you are then . . . off visiting Father Christmas?

MARJE *says nothing.*

None of my business anyway, is it love, really? None of my business. I'm married, separated now. My husband sells jeans back off Hoxford Hall (*She points to her jeans.*) Designer jeans, I can get you a pair if you like, wholesale . . . fixed all the girls up with them . . . only got a couple left. Don't tell her.

NORAH: Norah?

JESS: No, don't tell Norah.

A long silence. JESS *smokes.*

Don't mind me sitting here?

MARJE: No, not at all.

JESS: Nothing much on tonight. . . . Nancy let you make a cup of tea ask her nice.

MARJE: Nancy?

JESS: Woman what gave you the keys.

MARJE: Oh, I don't think I've met her.

JESS: You don't know Nancy?

MARJE: No.

JESS: That's good. Me and her don't get on, see.

MARJE: No?

JESS: No.

Pause.

So you don't know anyone then, girl?

Blackout.

Marje's journey to the common

Sound tape: which continues into the scene. A pub at closing time. Men's voices which fade into women's footsteps, then silence.
Lights up. In a spotlight centre-stage, MARJE wearing a coat, carrying a bag.

MARJE (*whispering*): From the corner, men call after us and for a while the obscenities seem to hang in the air like icicles, but we are deaf and dumb now in the dark night.

On one side, commonland, parkland, flat and black, here, Victorian terraces, gateposts, clipped privet hedges and curly wrought iron.

There's a gap in the curtains! I can see a man and a woman watching television. . . .

I only wanted ordinary things. A little house to live in, a garden, three square meals a day for my kids, a holiday now and then. My father wanted me to work in a bank. That was his ambition for me, to be a teller – on a High Street – somewhere.

. . . Under the railway arches she stops, leans back into the blackness, slips off a shoe and tips out a pile of shiny grey shale. Behind her – 'Andy loves Elaine', 'Ban the Bomb', 'Blacks Go Home', 'Skins Rule' – there is the sweet, damp, fungal smell of humanity. We are safe here.

She is fumbling in her bag for her cigarettes and a match . . . sulphur!

Old Sal'd do it for a packet of filter tips, that's what they said. She had hair the colour of cornflakes and lipstick that turned blue and every Friday I'd run errands for her. Two pounds of pigs' liver for her two dogs, Mark and John – Mark and John, the same names as her two dead babies.

Through the railway arches she is turning from the path, and we make our way through undergrowth. In the moonlight the winter trees are like old men's arms – spiteful, they scratch and prod.

We are in the middle of a forest.
. . . Nature . . . I hate nature. . . .
It frightens me. Towns are safe, houses are safe, streets are safe, shops are safe.

They knocked down the back to backs. The people left, and in the cracks grew the twitch grass, the long thistles, nettles, the hollyhocks, the dandelions and the daisies and then came the ants and the spiders, slugs and the slow-worms, the frogs and the tadpoles.

David Bradbury – the 'naughtiest boy in the school' – drank a tadpole out of a school milk bottle. In hospital they cut him open and a great blue toad jumped out.

At last, we have beaten the trees.
At last, the forest is behind us.
At last, high up on the skyline great houses with gardens that lean down to the commonland. . . .
. . . And the snore of traffic from the high, wide road.

Wandsworth Common

Night-time. MARJE and JESS.
Lights up.

JESS (*she has a can of Carlsberg Special*): I'd like to be an HGV driver – you know, heavy goods. I've a friend who does it – takes her everywhere – Amsterdam, Belgium, Denmark, Rotterdam . . . wouldn't believe it would you, a woman doing that? . . . We can do anything nowadays, can't we? Equal opportunities they call it. Did you know that?

MARJE: Yes . . . yes, I did.

JESS: Only I don't know how to go about getting my licence, see. That's my problem.

Slight pause.

I could ask her I suppose. I'd be happy doing that.

A long pause.

Quiet, aren't you?

MARJE: I'm sorry?

JESS: Don't worry, I'd rather you were quiet. Pat, that one in the caf, she's a talker, s'truth get a sore earhole standing next to her all night.
    . . . Still, she's all right. We're the only ones left here now, me and her. Used to be loads of girls . . . all moved down here when they cleaned out the square, see.

MARJE: Square?

JESS: Argyle Square. You don't know much do you? Couldn't go round the Square get a pint of milk without being lifted one time. I only went out to get a 50p for my electric and they took me in. I wasn't working, I swear to God. My electric had gone. I wanted 50p, they had me in – charged me, everything. Course, when things calmed down most the girls went back . . . not me and Pat. We like it here, see. I don't know why. I think it reminds me of the country.

In the distance, laughing voices, a car door opening, the car sets off.

(*Looking at her watch – to herself:*) Kicking them out early tonight.

(*To* MARJE:) Lord Somebody-or-other's daughter, does a lot of entertaining, part of her job see. Sometimes, 3 o'clock in the morning, they're still at it. (*Confidentially:*) She's in publishing, he's in the city. (*Pause.*) How do I know? (*Smiles.*) Read the *Daily Mail*, don't I.
    . . . Next door – I don't know much about them.

(*Looking at the next house.*) Now he's interesting, very interesting. He's high up in religion, not a missionary exactly, but something very like it.

(*At the next house, pause, she smiles.*) Then there's my little firecracker. (*Pause.*) Ever so swanky, drives a Morgan, watch her gardening in the summer . . . lovely little bum.

Pause.

Course they don't like us. Lot of trouble in the beginning – got up a petition and everything.

Pause. She looks at MARJE.

Nice for you I reckon.

MARJE: I'm sorry?

JESS: Having me to clue you in.

MARJE: Yes, very nice.

JESS: What would you have done if you were on your own then?

MARJE: I don't know – just have walked around I suppose.

JESS: Jesus . . . Talk about sitting duck.

During this conversation a car has drawn up some way off and stopped, its engine running.

JESS: First of the night. You all right here on your own?

MARJE: Yes, I'm fine.

JESS: Do what I told you. You got nothing to worry about – they ain't got nothing your old man ain't got, and remember, don't let 'em know it's your first, or they'll have a party with you . . . all right?

MARJE: Yes.

JESS: Be back in a jif . . . honest.

See you.

JESS *goes.* MARJE *watches. From the opposite direction a shadow falls at her feet. She looks up.*

Blackout.

A tea stand

Sound tape: London traffic.
    Lights up: NORAH *is bundled up against the cold, many scarves, mitts, hat, etc. She drinks tea from a paper cup. The* MAN *behind the stand is doing a crossword.*

NORAH: . . . I bet your wife doesn't like you working nights eh?

Pause. The MAN *says nothing.*

I bet she doesn't.

Pause.

I bet she plays hell.

Pause.

(*Shivering:*) What time did you say it was again?

The MAN *says nothing.*

My husband used to work nights when

we were first married. Funny, even though next door had this bloody great Dobermann, even though my mother was only four doors down, I always felt . . . jumpy somehow.

MAN (*filling in the word at last . . . then looks at his watch*): Half past seven.

NORAH: Some people like being on their own – you pop in on my sister unexpected, you get the big freeze . . . Me, I like to be with people, feel people around me . . . friends . . . have a bit of a chin-wag . . . have a bit of a giggle.

Pause.

Half past seven. Is that all?

Pause.

MAN: You've got company.

NORAH: I thought you said he'd gone.

MAN: He's come back.

NORAH (*sneaking a look*): Jesus wept! What does he think he looks like? Why's he got sunglasses on? – It's drizzling.

MAN (*not looking up*): P'raps he thinks he's famous.

NORAH: Yeah – but for what?ˑ

Off – the MAN*'s voice calls to* NORAH.

(*Panicky:*) No way sunshine. (*Under her breath:*) I've got ambitions to pop off in my bed at ninety-five.

NORAH *drains her tea and hurries off in the direction of the light.*

MAN: Oy – station's that way.

NORAH: I'm going back to the boarding house. See if you can flog Wally a kebab.

Wandsworth Common. A railway bridge

MARJE *and* JOHNNY.
Lights up.

JOHNNY: No . . . no further. I don't like the dark.

MARJE *stops and looks at him.*

She won't follow us here, whatshername?

MARJE: Jess.

JOHNNY: Yeah, Jess. She won't follow us here. She's frightened of the policeman.

MARJE: What do you mean . . . policeman?

JOHNNY: Policeman. He has a fag here every night. He won't tonight.

MARJE: How do you know?

JOHNNY: Wednesday's his night off.

MARJE: Oh.

They both stand for some time.

JOHNNY: You said you'd lie down.

MARJE: Yes . . . I will.

Another pause. MARJE *makes to lie down.*

JOHNNY (*laughs delightedly*): You shouldn't do that yet. You have to ask for my money. You have to ask for my money . . . otherwise I could do a runner.

MARJE: That's right.

JOHNNY *gets out a large wallet and hands over two £5 notes.*

MARJE (*quietly*): I said £15.

JOHNNY *laughs again, hands over another £5 note.* MARJE *takes them, puts them in her bag. she makes to lie down.*

JOHNNY: You haven't given me a 'd'. I'll tell on you.

MARJE: Oh yes. (*She gets one out of her bag.*)

JOHNNY: You'll have to help me.

Blackout.

Sound: the very faint ticking of a clock.

Spotlight picks out MARJE*'s face . . . expressionless. She is on the ground.* JOHNNY *is on top of her but can hardly be seen.*

Ticking stops. MARJE *and* JOHNNY *relax. They lie there. After a minute* MARJE, *still expressionless automatically puts her arm around him, strokes his head . . . makes to kiss him.* JOHNNY *freezes, then starts up, pulling on his clothes.*

JOHNNY (*ferociously*): What's your game?

MARJE (*confused*): I'm sorry.

JOHNNY: You don't do that. That's not right.

MARJE: I didn't mean anything.

JOHNNY: What are you anyway?

MARJE: Nothing. I'm nothing.

JOHNNY: You do that and I'll tell on you. You'll get into trouble.

MARJE: I'm sorry. I forgot. I . . .

JOHNNY: You'll get in trouble if I tell on you. That's not right.

MARJE: Don't tell. I didn't mean it. I'm sorry. I forgot . . .!

Blackout.

Wandsworth Common

Sound tape: light footsteps along a stone path. They stop suddenly.
Lights up. MARJE is looking over the common . . . She sees something . . . secret . . . strange . . . and wonderful.
She is transfixed.
Blackout.

King's Cross guest house. Marje and Norah's room

Sound tape: the faint ticking of a clock.
Lights up.
Darkness, MARJE switches on a side lamp.

NORAH (*suddenly*): Who is it? Marje, is that you?

MARJE: Yes it's me, Norah.

NORAH (*propped up in bed, a coat around her shoulders*): Jesus wept. What's the time?

MARJE: Three o'clock.

NORAH: Three o'clock? How did you get back?

MARJE: A friend of Jess's gave us a lift.

NORAH: Oh yeah – who'd that be? Dracula?

Pause.

I've been worried sick about you.

MARJE (*sits on her own bed*): I know, I'm sorry.

NORAH: Well . . .?

MARJE: Well what?

NORAH: Well . . . How did it go? Did you . . . you know, did you go through with it?

MARJE says nothing.

Oh come on Marje, I've been thinking about nothing else all evening. Put me out of my misery for God's sake.

MARJE: I'll talk to you tomorrow Norah, I promise, only I'm too tired now. I think I'll have a bath.

NORAH: You'll be lucky.

MARJE: Why?

NORAH: No hot water. The only hot water on this floor comes out of Lynda's sink, jammy bugger.

Pause.

Look. Are you all right?

MARJE: Yes. I'm just very cold.

NORAH *rummages under the bedclothes, takes out a hot water bottle and throws it to* MARJE.

MARJE *half lies down on the bed.*

Silence.

NORAH: Oh for Christ's sake Marje, say something.

MARJE: Not now Norah. tomorrow, please. I will talk tomorrow.

A long silence.

NORAH (*very quietly*): Look Marje, let's go home eh? I've had a chance to look round now, and quite honestly this London business is very overrated . . . Oh, yes, if you're a Yank . . . pots of money, sure you can have a good time . . . well . . . apart from anything else, it's bloody freezing . . .

Pause.

We were mad to think we could try it in the first place – if you ask me. I mean, we're just ordinary women you and me, we're not cut out for . . . What do you say then, eh?

MARJE *says nothing.*

I've done a lot of thinking and quite frankly I'm not sure I could do it with someone I didn't fancy. I mean all right . . . I do fancy a lot of men. Well, variety's the spice and all that . . . I mean, I have with a couple of men I didn't exactly fancy, but that was when Mickie went off it that time and I went a bit mental.

Pause.

Don't get me wrong. I'm not saying I wouldn't do it. I mean let's face it if someone walked in now and said I'll give you £100 for a quickie I'd probably say all right . . . fair enough, providing he didn't look like the Elephant Man, but it's not as simple as that is it? It's a whole world you and me know nothing about.

Outside the room, footsteps, quick, and light. The next door opens, seconds later the sound of something being lugged, then a tap at the door.

LYNDA: Norah? Are you awake? Can I come in?

NORAH: Yes, come in . . . it's only three o'clock at night.

LYNDA enters. She lugs a suitcase behind her. She is dressed for night-clubbing.

They both whisper.

Where've you been?

LYNDA: It's not where I've been, Norah my love, it's where I'm going.

NORAH: All right, where are you going?

LYNDA: Guess.

NORAH: Albert Hall.

LYNDA: The Hilton, my dear, that's all.

NORAH: Jesus.

LYNDA: I've struck lucky. I knew I would. I just didn't think it would be this quick. (*She giggles.*);

NORAH: Oh yeah.

LYNDA is undressing, selecting a new outfit from the suitcase.

LYNDA: I went to a club tonight . . . got a tip off they might be looking for new girls . . . (*She stops.*) Look, I didn't hold out on you two, honest, it just didn't seem your sort of place.

NORAH: Go on . . .

LYNDA (*very excited*): Anyway – I'd not taken me coat off and sat down five minutes, when this bloke comes over, foreign, well more French . . . nicely spoken, with that quiffy hair and a lovely dark navy suit on, well we really hit it off, talked about everything under the sun, world cup, politics, you name it, so there we are, nineteen to the dozen, like we've known each other all our lives, and this tall woman comes over, says there's no point in waiting any longer cos the boss has got laid up and could I come back tomorrow morning, and before I've time to knock back my Pernod and coke,this bloke's offering me a lift home.

NORAH: Where is he now?

LYNDA: Parked on the corner in his BMW X Reg.

Long pause – NORAH explodes.

NORAH: Well friggin! – fuckin! – frig!

LYNDA: What's up?

NORAH: That's brilliant that isn't it, eh? That's effing brilliant. I don't believe it, I don't believe this is happening. You're knocking back Pernods, getting chatted up by hunky Frenchmen, . . . (*Hissing in the direction of the now apparently sleeping* MARJE:) . . . She's trolling around London in her best coat, playing at being Madame Sin, and there's me, stuck in here on my own all night . . . with (*She gets a book from the bed and flings it at* LYNDA.) daft bloody books.

LYNDA (*picks it up*): Lord Baden Powell – A Lifetime's Memoirs. It'll be a good book that – very educational. You'll find out how to start your own scout group.

NORAH: I'm pig sick.

LYNDA (*still dressing*): Well look Norah, I'm going to that interview tomorrow, if I get the job I'll put in a good word for you with the boss, I'll say you're mature but eager . . .

NORAH: Oh, hark at her, 'mature'.

You make me sound like a pair of sweaty socks. Past it, you mean. Anyway, hang on a minute, just hang on one little minute, unless I'm much mistaken that was my hot selling point, 'They don't like dolly birds, Norah, makes them uncomfortable, with your big hooter and varicose veins, you'll be raking it in' . . .

LYNDA: As I was saying, when I meet the boss tomorrow morning, I'll put in a good word. Now fair dos – what do you say?

NORAH (*pause*): Stuff yourself.

LYNDA (*now in a decent skirt and blouse, hair brushed and less make up*): Right, that's me done. How do I look?

NORAH (*miserably*): Like Mary O'Hara.

LYNDA *is about to shut the suitcase.*

Listen Lynd, these foreign men, they're, you know – a bit kinky – go in for all sorts – things you've never dreamed of – doubles, trebles – how about (*She dives into the suitcase.*) I put one of your frocks on see – brush my hair forward, over my face – you can tell him I'm your big sister – he'll be creaming himself – tell you what, we'll split it 60–40.

LYNDA (*shutting the suitcase*): No thanks, Norah. I don't think he's that type.

(*Ready to leave:*) Is Marje asleep? Why she got all her clothes on?

NORAH (*miserably*): Old northern custom.

LYNDA (*hesitating*): Look, I won't do this again, right, cos we agreed didn't we – every man for himself, but, well there you are. (*She takes a couple of tenners and hands them to* NORAH.) Give one to Marje. Never again mind, just tonight – cos my luck's changed.

The Chancery

Lights up. Bright, cold early morning. A desk. ALISTAIR *is filling in a form. He is young, conservatively dressed, almost the young executive. Opposite him is* LYNDA.

ALISTAIR: . . . And finally, have you a criminal record?

LYNDA *hesitates, slightly shocked.*

LYNDA: No . . . no I haven't.

ALISTAIR: Right . . . (*Throwing down his pen, he rises and starts to pace about . . . hands in pockets.*) Well, we're right in the heart of the city, Lynda here. (*He laughs.*) Big Bang country. You probably noticed Lloyds opposite, Inns of Court down the road, five hundred members, five hundred or there abouts, mainly City types, but weekend, fair amount of foreigners, foreign business men. . . . (*He stops.*) Is it me, or is it freezing in here?

LYNDA: Well it's . . .

ALISTAIR: It's not warm is it?

LYNDA: No it's . . .

ALISTAIR: It's all right if you're in and out . . . (*Taking off his suit jacket, gloomily reaching for a pullover:*) . . . but I was stuck in here all day yesterday.

LYNDA: It is chilly, I must say.

ALISTAIR: And that's something coming from a northerner. My wife's a northern lassie like yourself, from Keighley. (*A little smile.*) Skins like rhinoceros up there. (*He takes a wine list and tosses it matily to* LYNDA.) What's your favourite champagne, Lynda – Do you know?

LYNDA: Favourite? My favourite?

ALISTAIR: Mmm. Dom Perignon, Veuve Cliquot, Moet et Chandon?

LYNDA: Er . . . I didn't really know there were different makes.

ALISTAIR: The password here at the Chancery, Lynda, is 'Spend'. (*He lowers his voice.*) The theory being, the more a gentleman invests early on in the evening, the higher the dividend at the end.

He sits.

And that's supposed to keep us both happy.

LYNDA (*still studying the winelist*): Well the Boll . . .

ALISTAIR: Bollinger it is then. So, let's

suppose you're settled with a member, one of the old boys say, sipping chilled Bollinger in a nice warm little corner. (*He tosses* LYNDA *the menu.*) What about nosh? You're not a vegetarian I suppose?

LYNDA: No.

ALISTAIR: Only we've had a few of them lately. It's not me you understand. I don't give a monkey's left bollock. It's him. (*He thumbs upstairs.*) Doesn't like it.

LYNDA: No I'm not a veg . . .

ALISTAIR: What about starters – see anything you fancy?

LYNDA *studies the menu.*

ALISTAIR (*picking his teeth*): Remember the old password!

LYNDA: Salmon bruillé.

ALISTAIR: Good, main course?

LYNDA: Rump steak.

ALISTAIR: Mmm, nice and rare.

LYNDA: With sauté potatoes, beans and buttered asparagus.

ALISTAIR: Asparagus is back on is it? And desert? A few fresh lychees.

LYNDA (*pleased with herself*): A few fresh lychees with fresh cream.

ALISTAIR: Well done, Lynda. (*Shivering.*) That sounds very appetising.

King's Cross guest house. Norah and Marje's room.

Lights up.
    NORAH *and* MARJE *sit on the beds. They drink coffee out of a thermos flask, sharing a cup. It is early afternoon. Sunshine streams into the room.*

MARJE: He asked me how much and I told him. He said here was too near the road and he pointed over the croft to the railway bridge. The grass was damp and squelchy. We walked in a crocodile, me leading the way.

NORAH: Weren't you frightened?

MARJE (*thinks*): No . . . I wasn't frightened . . . To get to the railway

arches you have to go through this . . . wood . . . a cloud must have passed over the moon . . . for a few seconds it was pitch black . . . I heard him breathe. It was then I first realised.

NORAH: What?

MARJE: That he was frightened of me . . .

Pause.

NORAH: Let's go home, Marje.

MARJE: No . . . not yet.

NORAH: Why? I know you. You're not cut out for this.

MARJE *goes to her bag and gets out money, in notes and silver.*

NORAH: There were others?

MARJE: I've worked it out. We've ten days left. If I make more or less the same every night till we leave I'll have paid the electric and I'll have £80 left – I can make some sort of Christmas with that for Del and the kids . . . and then I'm straight. It's a new year and a fresh start . . . don't you see?

Pause.

NORAH: How did you go through with it? (*Softly.*) How did you go through with it?

MARJE: It wasn't that bad. (*Pause, very softly.*) Something else happened. It must have been about two o'clock. I'd kept to the footpath this time – I was almost back by the big houses, when I saw something come out of the gardens . . . I knew it wasn't a dog or a cat . . . I don't know how . . . I saw it cross the road, sniff the air and bound off across the far side of the common . . . It was a fox . . . I've never seen a real one . . . but a fox! – There in the middle of the road, with houses, cars and lampposts. . . .

NORAH: It couldn't have been.

MARJE: Why?

NORAH: Well, they're extinct in this country.

MARJE: Are they heck!

NORAH: Well they are in London . . . You only get foxes in forests . . . or zoos.

MARJE: No, when Jess came back I told her I'd seen a fox, and she said there'd been hundreds all over the common, that when they'd built the big new road the foxes had dug their lairs in the gardens of the big houses and that one night men had come and laid traps and now only a few foxes were left . . . and there were still traps, traps set all over the common.

Blackout.

Wandsworth Common. Night

Lights up.
    MARJE *is leaning against a wall. She is sweating. She breathes deeply. She stands up. From an inside pocket she takes out a handful of notes, she counts them, then replaces them. For a few moments she is very still, looking out over the wide commonland.*
    From under a hedge she drags out a shopping bag. Inside is a parcel wrapped in a plastic bag. Ceremoniously she lays out the bag like a table cloth on the soil and slowly unwraps the parcel. It is offal, scrag end, cheapest cuts of butcher's meat. She takes some moments arranging it to her satisfaction. She stands – looks out over the common, then backs off and walks away into the shadows.

Blackout.

Interval.

The Chancery. Ladies' toilet

Sound tape: outside in the club, loud music . . . people are laughing and talking.
    Lights up.
    LYNDA *sits on a pouff in front of a mirror. She is trying to repair her make-up. She feels ill. Her hand is unsteady.*
    CARESS *enters; a burst of sound.*

CARESS: If I don't do something with these legs soon I'll go mad.

She starts to take off her stockings. Out of her handbag she takes some lotion. She smells it.

This will make me popular.

She dabs the stuff on to her legs. She takes in LYNDA.

Your first night?

LYNDA: Yes.

CARESS: You don't have to drink it all, you know.

LYNDA: I'm sorry?

CARESS: The champagne . . . you don't have to drink it all . . . You can tip it.

LYNDA: Tip it?

CARESS (*she picks up* LYNDA's *glass and tips it on to the floor*): All the girls do it. Why do you think the carpets are squelchy?

LYNDA: I did wonder.

CARESS: You'll end up with these I'm afraid . . . champagne fleas . . . they live in the carpet . . . Night after night you see. Never a chance to dry out.

She looks at her legs. They are now covered in white lotion.

I'm going to have my work cut out explaining that later . . ..

She puts her stockings back on.

You going case with that bloke?

LYNDA: Er . . .

CARESS: Going case . . . it's an expression you'll hear all the time here. It means going back to his hotel . . . dates back to when the girls had to take overnight cases with them otherwise they couldn't get into the hotel.

LYNDA: Oh!

CARESS: Don't mind me, I'm a mine of useless information.

LYNDA: No . . . that's interesting.

CARESS: I thought so . . .. Well . . .?

LYNDA: Sorry?

CARESS: Are you?

LYNDA: I don't know.

CARESS: Well you'd better find out soon. If he's not . . . you'll only get a tenner, you know.

LYNDA: A tenner?

CARESS: Didn't they tell you?

LYNDA: No.

CARESS: You sit down at a table – you get a hostess fee – that's £10, right . . . But if you sit down with a bloke all night and he doesn't 'go case', that's all you get . . . all evening. If he's not interested you'd best ditch him. Try your luck elsewhere.

LYNDA: I think he is . . . interested in er . . . 'going case'.

CARESS: What's his hotel?

LYNDA: I don't know.

CARESS: Didn't Paula tell you?

LYNDA: No.

CARESS: Look, you've got to find out what hotel he's staying in . . . some just aren't any good.

LYNDA: Why?

CARESS: Security . . . You might get in, but you'll never get out unless he's a gentleman of course and he escorts you to the door, but they're few and far between.

LYNDA: No, nobody said anything.

CARESS: Never go back to The Cumberland – there's a pervert on the door gets a kick out of taking girls' pictures and handing them in at the cop shop . . . The Savoy . . . Inn on the Park . . . Hilton . . . Dorchester . . . they're usually all right – Mayfair he has to have booked a double room, otherwise they'll have him and you.

LYNDA: Thanks . . . er . . .

CARESS: Caress.

Blackout.

King's Cross Station buffet. Mid-morning

Sound tape: a café after the rush hour. Station noises in the background.
Lights up.
NORAH *has a can of coke in front of her. In her bag she has a bottle of vodka which she's been pouring into the can.*
NORAH *is nodding. She is just about to drop off to sleep.*

STAN: Wouldn't do that, girl.

NORAH *(startled)*: What?

STAN *(sliding into the seat opposite. He has a cup of coffee)*: Drop off like that . . . See Ethel over there. *(He points to the food counter.)* She's had her eyes on you. You drop off she'll have a copper here 'fore you can say 'cheese roll'.

NORAH: What for?

STAN: Loitering for one thing – but that would only be for starters . . . Make a lot of trouble for you . . . Don't want that do we . . . nice girl like you.

NORAH: I can sit here and have a can of coke, can't I? It's a free country.

STAN: Matter of opinion, that love.

NORAH *(in the direction of* ETHEL*)*: Nosy bitch! What's it to her anyway? And what's it to you, mister?

STAN: Don't mind me. Just trying to save you bother that's all.

Pause. STAN *drinks.*

You're new, aren't you?

NORAH: What do you mean?

STAN: Haven't seen you around here before. I know most of the girls on the station.

NORAH: Oh do you? Well you don't know me, right.

STAN *(he points)*: That's where I work . . . heel bar.

NORAH: Oh yeah.

STAN: Gerrard's. Didn't have to work there. They got heel bars all over London, but I asked to work here cos I like stations.

NORAH: Oh yeah.

STAN: Well trains really, but stations can be interesting places.

NORAH *(looking round)*: Fascinating.

STAN: Oh not these places, the . . . er . . . superstructures. For example, King's Cross was the first station in Europe. I think, to actually look like a station.

Pause.

NORAH *(stupified)*: Hadn't you better get back to your heel bar?

STAN: No, I've a lad in there. Anyway I take my lunch now, see, when it's quiet.

NORAH: Nice when it's quiet, isn't it?

Pause.

STAN: You're not waiting for a train.

NORAH: How do you know?

STAN: I saw you come in. You, me and the old girl in the corner, we're the only ones in here not waiting for a train.

NORAH: How do you know?

STAN: Don't know really. I come in here every day for my lunch – sort of got a feel for it by now.

NORAH: Oh yeah. (*Yawning.*)

STAN: Am I boring you?

NORAH: I'm knackered if you must know. I've been up half the night.

STAN: Yes?

NORAH: Talking.

STAN: Of course.

NORAH (*hissing*): Look, I don't know what's going through your nasty little mind, but let's get one thing straight shall we. I'm here on holiday with a friend, to see London, a little pre-Christmas break. Have a butchers at the fairy lights. . . . All right. Have we got that straight?

STAN (*embarrassed*): Don't mind me, I er, didn't mean no offence.

NORAH (*huffy*): Yeah, well none taken I suppose. (*She reads.*)

STAN (*good humoured*): Good book?

NORAH: Yeah, it is actually. It's, er, very educational.

STAN: Are you a student then?

NORAH (*pleased*): Yeah – you could say that, a mature student.

STAN: What's your subject?

NORAH: Eh?

STAN: What are you studying?

NORAH *shows him the book.*

STAN: Ah 'Kantankye'.

NORAH: I beg your pardon.

STAN: Kantankye – that's what the natives used to call Lord Baden Powell, means 'He of the big hat'.

Pause.

NORAH (*put out*): Yeah well I haven't got to that bit yet, this bit I'm on at the moment he's trying to advise his best friend, this young lad, right, his old man's died, left all his money to his older brother, he can't decide whether to go on a once-in-a-lifetime safari to deepest Africa, or stay at home, marry Miss E. Moscrop, spinster of the parish, and take the cloth.

STAN: What do you think he should do?

NORAH: Marry the old biddy, she's loaded.

STAN *laughs.*

NORAH (*swigging her coke – in the direction of* ETHEL): I'm going over there and sneeze all over her scrambled eggs.

STAN: No, look, let me buy you a coffee.

NORAH: Won't that reaffirm Ethel, 'Queen of the Hot Plate's' hunch, I'm here for immoral purposes?

STAN: Probably.

NORAH: All right, if it gets up Ethel's nose I'll have a coffee and a cream doughnut.

STAN: Coming up.

NORAH (*straight at* ETHEL): No . . . make that an éclair.

Blackout.

Wandsworth Common

Lights up. MARJE *is looking out over the common. She is watching the fox.*

MARJE (*whispering*): Hungry, little fox? . . . Scrag end . . . back end . . . offal . . . neck bone . . . gizzard . . . giblets . . .
  I can see your breath! I can see your breath! Sweet and smoky in the moonlight . . .
  Are you alone, mmm? No mate? Cubs? Mmm?

Pause.

Are you alone?

Pause. From inside the house, two voices, a door opens, they walk up the drive. MARJE *watches, fearful.*

Look at you. . . . Go on . . . go on . . . don't stand there, what are you waiting for, run, run, under the hedge, over the common, quick . . . quick.

More voices, laughter and goodbyes, eventually the car door slams. The car drives away . . . footsteps . . . a door closes. MARJE *relaxes.*

The fox turns to look at MARJE.

You were lucky, that's all. But what about next time? You're too near the house, too near the glass – they never draw their curtains. You can see the light shining all the way across the common. One day they'll look out and see you, they'll send for the men and that'll be it. . . . Game up.

Why not the other houses, dark and quiet, people away, the gardens overgrown and wild? Why stay here by the cars and the common? Why? Why?

The fox turns to look at the house.

Are you watching them? Is that it?
Are you watching them, little fox. Why?

MARJE *turns and she too watches the house.*

Why?

A twig snaps somewhere close. MARJE *jumps.*

MARJE (*to the fox*): Yes I heard it. Jess?

Pause.

MARJE *looks at her watch.*

Too soon, too soon for Jess.

Another twig snaps.

Hello?

Pause, she listens till there is nothing but absolute silence.

No not this time.

The fox begins to feast again. She leans back, takes out notes and a handful of change.

Four tonight. The quiet man who walked across the common and called

me flower, spat on me, another puked up at my feet, another sobbed, another swore. They all pinch, push, prick, poke, tear, twist, bend, that's what they pay for.

I can't remember their faces, little fox. I can't remember their faces in the moonlight.

Do you know what I remember most, out of the dark, damp nights, their smell . . .. I remember their smell.

Blackout.

The Chancery

Sound tape: a packed nightclub.
Lights up. LYNDA *and* CARESS *are giving* DESMOND *a discreet 'hand job' under the table. It should not be immediately obvious.*
They take turns . . . at the moment CARESS *is operating.* LYNDA *acts as lookout.* DESMOND *is an Afrikana.*

DESMOND (*pissed*): . . . I'm not joking, you could count the peas on your plate, little lamb chop . . . tiny little chap he was, almost brought a lump to my throat.

LYNDA: Desmond . . .

DESMOND: Looked like he'd died of exposure . . . What's that on the side of my plate I asks . . .. That, sir? Mint sauce he says. Mint sauce, I says, first time I seen mint sauce with a shine on it.

LYNDA: Desmond . . .

DESMOND: Sure it's not fried snot.

CARESS (*sighing, taking her hand from under the table, flexing her fingers a little*): I'm sorry I'm going to have to stop a minute, I'm getting cramp.

LYNDA (*as if to a five-year-old*): You're going to have to concentrate a bit for us Desmond.

DESMOND *reaches for his drink.* LYNDA *puts a firm hand over the glass.*

No more bubbles till you've been a good boy for us, Desmond.

DESMOND (*petulantly*): Two hundred pounds is a lot of money.

LYNDA: Not for a man with all your investments . . . your sheep farm, your cattle ranch.

CARESS: Your hamburger stall, your ice cream emporium . . . your patented lather-in-sea-water soap on a rope, your jelly bean sandals.

DESMOND: No I suppose not, eh?

He takes CARESS's *hand and slaps it back on to his crutch.*

Not for a big man like me eh?

DESMOND *flinches.*

LYNDA: Just to your left, Desmond, do you see it . . . two doors down.

DESMOND *sees to his clothing and, with difficulty, stands.*

CARESS: Don't fall over the step, bang your head on the bog door and crack your head open will you, Desmond?

DESMOND (*pleasantly*): Don't worry, ladies. (*He wiggles his crutch.*) Back in two shakes of a lamb's tail.

He goes.

CARESS: It's not worth it.

LYNDA: You're joking, aren't you? He's got a grand on him in readies.

CARESS: If they catch us we'll get suspended, you know that don't you?

LYNDA: They won't catch us. (*She nods in the direction of Oscar.*) He's got pals in tonight . . . He's socialising. We're all right.

LYNDA *sits back in the chair and sways gently to the music.* CARESS *watches her, then she too looks around the club. Suddenly she drains her glass and stands up.*

CARESS: Fuck it . . . I'm off.

LYNDA: You what?

CARESS: I'm sorry, I haven't got the stomach for it tonight.

LYNDA: What about Oscar?

CARESS: Fuck Oscar.

LYNDA: But you can't go now I've set it all up. You've got a stake in it. It's a hundred quid for easy peasy. You'd be a mug to go now.

DESMOND (*lurching back*): Would you credit it? You can't go anywhere in this blasted country, one of those nippy little wine waiters giving me the eye in the Gent's Boudoir.

LYNDA (*looking at* CARESS, *helping* DESMOND *into his seat*): Are you nice and cosy, Desmond?

DESMOND *nods petulantly.* CARESS *sighs and sits down.*

DESMOND: Pretended he was drying his hands. I saw him rubbing himself against the paper towel dispenser.

LYNDA (*hand under the table, discreetly unzipping* DESMOND): Because you've got to help us out now, Desmond eh? You've got to . . . (*She stops . . . she shares a look of pleasant surprise with* CARESS.) That's a better boy Desmond.

DESMOND: Wouldn't take his eyes off me . . . nippy little fella . . . made a suggestive noise too when I was leaving . . . sort of wheeze.

DESMOND *is beginning to get seriously aroused.*

Course it's the public-school system I blame, all those bender headmasters . . .. I read in *The Star*, I think it was, only yesterday, Geography teacher made this kid, poor little soul, only about fifteen he was, bend over . . . bend over (*He breathes heavily.*) one of those poshy public schools . . .. Pants down, no, I mean kex and everything, bare botty poor little soul.

He breathes very heavily. CARESS *and* LYNDA *watch him expectantly. Long pause.*

CARESS: You were giving us your views on the British educational system.

Blackout.

King's Cross guest house

Sound tape: the ticking of a clock. Lights up. MARJE's *face in the moonlight. She is in bed. Her eyes are open. She listens. In the darkness* NORAH *and* LYNDA *are shapes against the window. They whisper.*

NORAH: Just shut it.

LYNDA: Oh come on Norah, even you

can see the funny side – I remember
her turning beetroot if a bloke winked
at her.

NORAH: Well I don't like it, I don't like
it at all.

LYNDA (*stifling giggles*): No – but she
obviously does.

NORAH (*furious*): I won't tell you again
– keep that dirty little mouth of yours
shut.

LYNDA: Sorry Norah, I forgot, you're a
born again virgin aren't you, since you
hit the Big Smoke.

Uneasy pause.

How are you fixed at the
minute?

NORAH: Fixed?

LYNDA: For cash.

Pause.

NORAH: All right.

LYNDA: Don't make me laugh – you're
skint, I know you are.

NORAH: I'll manage – till we get home
– I'll manage somehow.

LYNDA: And then what?

Pause.

Eh? And then what? We're not
here on a works weekend. The whole
point of this trip is that we go home
with more than we came.

Pause.

So?

Pause.

What you going to do then?

NORAH (*rounding on her, suddenly
furious – she turns into the
moonlight*): I don't know what I'm going to do. I
don't know anything anymore – all
right?

Silence.

LYNDA (*gently*): Look I'll get tomorrow
night off the club and I'll take you out
with me, eh? We'll go out together, the
two of us. What do you say?

NORAH: I'll think about it.

LYNDA: Don't do me any favours.

NORAH (*suddenly*): Maybe I don't need
your help. Maybe you don't know
everything after all. Maybe I've got
plans of my own.

Pause.

There's more than one way to skin a
rabbit.

Blackout.

King's Cross buffet

*Sound tape: café noises, carol singers on
the station.*
   Lights up. NORAH *is sat at a table.*
There are two coffees and two cakes.
   STAN *arrives, a little breathless.*

STAN: Good morning.

   NORAH *engrossed in a book doesn't
   hear.*

(*He coughs:*) Good morning.

NORAH (*looking up*): Oh hello . . . .
You're just in time. I thought elevenses
better be on me for a change.

STAN (*he sits*): That's kind, Norah, very
kind. I'm sorry about yesterday, I
couldn't get away, you should have
come in the shop.

NORAH: No . . . I could see you were
busy.

STAN: Where did you go?

NORAH: Oh you know . . . back to the
hotel. (*She turns the corner of her
book and puts it in her bag.*)

STAN: How's your studying?

NORAH (*blankly*): Me what?

STAN: Your . . .

NORAH: Oh my studies. (*Bleakly:*) Not
too bad. I'm on a chapter on hog-
hunting at the moment.

STAN: Hog-hunting?

NORAH: Mmm, apparently the officers
got up to it out in India. I haven't
finished the chapter yet but it's a bit
like polo only with hogs.

*Carol singers become particularly
'Jubilato'.*

Jesus wept . . . (*Turning, loudly:*) Give
'em a tanner someone, tell 'em shove
off.

Pause. STAN *drinks his coffee. He watches* NORAH.

STAN: How's your friend?

NORAH: What friend? Oh her . . . (*She shrugs.*) I don't know. She's hardly opened her gob past couple of days.

STAN: You and Ethel seem to have made it up.

NORAH: Me and Ethel – we're bosom pals. There's nothing I couldn't tell you about Ethel. Did you know her husband played inside right for Tottenham Hotspur in 1945? And her Great-aunt Vi left £50 to the Battersea Dogs' Home?

STAN: So you're still not enjoying it then?

NORAH: What?

STAN: Your . . . holiday.

NORAH: Oh yeah, well it's every girl's dream isn't it? . . . a fortnight in the buffet at King's Cross.

STAN: You'll be going home soon.

NORAH: Can't be soon enough for me.

STAN: It's a shame.

NORAH: What is?

STAN: You've been here all this time and you haven't seen more of London . . . seen the sights.

NORAH: I've seen Ethel.

Blackout.

Wandsworth Common

Lights up. MARJE *is with a smartly dressed middle-aged man. She appears ill at ease.*

MAN (*offering* MARJE *a cigarette; she refuses*): . . . it spread to his ears in the end so we had to have him put down, but I missed it, see, come nine o'clock there I'd be, sat in the old armchair, fingers drumming, so my wife says go out anyway, just for the walk, good exercise you see, better than all this bleeding jogging they get up to – so I started coming down anyway. (*Pause.*) Course can hardly move in the summer for courting couples, not this time of year though eh . . . freeze their 'willie-wonkers' (*He laughs.*) . . . know what I mean?

Pause.

Business good is it?

MARJE *shrugs and turns away.*

Not being nosy or nothing – just wondered, just wondered. (*Pause.*) Wouldn't catch me paying for it. No way, lady. Got a nice little wife I have – get all that free plus my washing and my dinners . . . I could send her down here and she'd earn me a small fortune – right little gold mine she'd be, not that I would, mind – cos I love her see. (*Pause.*) She's a good little girl, decent, know what I mean, decent clean living girl – goes to church and everything. (*Pause.*) Now my first wife – right slag she was.

He stops and looks at her.

MARJE (*softly*): Look I don't mean to be funny or anything but if you're not . . . p'raps you could move on – only you being here isn't helpful.

Pause.

MAN: Oh stone me – not helpful, eh? Well, what would be helpful?

MARJE: If you went.

MAN (*quietly*): You got a cheek, ain't you? (*Pause.*) That's rather an unpleasant remark, do you know that? This common belongs to everyone see. I got as much right here as you. You got no more right here than me. I got more right see, cos I'm a resident of this borough, I live here, I'm a regular common user. You're breaking the law you are – I'm a law abiding citizen.

He moves off in a huff. He stops, lights a cigarette, then walks back to MARJE.

I was being nice to you, do you know that, talking to you, you should be thankful a decent person takes the time to speak to you – to have a conversation with scum like you.

Lights down.

In the blackout

Voices off.

MAN (*wearily*): Well there's nothing there now. Probably kids.

Lights partially up. MARJE is centre-stage, crouched, hiding. Her face is bleeding. She holds her stomach.

WOMAN: No . . . not at this time of night.

MAN (*yawning*): Morning.

WOMAN: What?

MAN: I said it's . . .

WOMAN: Look, there.

MAN: Where?

WOMAN: There, look do you see it?

MARJE *cringes.*

MAN: I can't see anything . . . where? . . .. It's a bush.

They laugh softly.

WOMAN: Well I heard something.

Their voices fade as they go back into the house. MARJE relaxes.

(*Yawning*): Could have been one of those wretched women.

WOMAN: No it sounded like . . .

MAN: What?

The contents of MARJE's bag have spilled open. She sits up, feels her mouth, straightens her coat, she starts to put things back in her bag, she hears something and looks up..

MARJE (*pause . . . softly*): There you are . . .. There you are . . .

Blackout.

London at night

Sound tape: London traffic.
Lights up. NORAH and STAN are on top of an open double-decker bus with a hoard of adolescent Chinese. NORAH wears a plastic Union Jack boater.
They raise their voices to be heard over the wind, traffic, chatter.

STAN: . . . Course that was the trams . . . the first double-decker bus as we know it was not until 1933 . . .

NORAH (*very excited, pointing ahead*): . . . I recognise that, Stanley. I've seen that on *News at Ten* . . .

STAN: . . . Passengers refused to go upstairs at the start, they were afraid they'd fall off . . . .

NORAH: . . . Trafalgar Square, all the pigeons, look see . . .

STAN: . . . Course a lot of the roads were still cobbled . . .

NORAH: . . . And that's Nelson's column. They've got the look . . . (*She leans back.*) It's like another world . . .

STAN: . . . I'm sorry Norah, I didn't quite catch that.

NORAH (*shouting*): . . . All the people, the shops open . . . all the famous statues and buildings.

STAN: It wasn't always like this . . . see that building there?

NORAH (*looking down*): Yes.

STAN: One of the most respected banks in Europe, when they dug the foundations in the last century, they found the largest number of prehistoric fossils in any one part of the United Kingdom.

NORAH: What do you mean?

STAN: Bones of great cave bears, lions and massive long-haired tigers.

NORAH: What, in Trafalgar Square?

STAN (*grinning*): A million years ago.

NORAH: Give over. (*She jumps up, very excited.*) Look, look, that punky lad, he's jumped in the fountain – look, look, there's another one.

NORAH *points them out to the other passengers.*

And another.

There is a great gabble of Chinese voices – laughter.

They're all in now, look, they're all in.

There is polite applause for the punks from the Chinese.

NORAH *leans back, laughing.*

STAN: Are you cold?

NORAH: Not as cold as them.

Pause. STAN is watching NORAH.

What's going on down there?

STAN: Where?

NORAH: That crowd, looks like bother – all the police and the cop cars.

STAN: That's where they do opera, Norah. It'll be a first night. All the knobs go to that.

NORAH: Come on Stan, let's do a bit of mingling.

Blackout.

The penthouse

Lights up. LYNDA *stands at a window. A* MAN *enters. He wears expensive casual clothes. She turns.*

MAN: . . . a bit like looking down at an anthill . . .. (*He pours himself a drink.*) The view from the other side is said to be more distinguished, but that's Traitor's Gate you can see a little way off so I like to think our view is the more atmospheric.

Pause.

Is anything the matter? (LYNDA *says nothing.*) You're staring at me.

LYNDA *turns back to the window.*

(*Brusquely*): Take your coat off.

LYNDA: I haven't made up my mind if I'm staying.

MAN (*irritable*): I see.

He sits.

LYNDA *looks around the flat.*

LYNDA: Do you live here on your own?

MAN (*hesitantly*): Yes, I do.

LYNDA: But at weekends you go back to the country?

MAN: Not always.

LYNDA: You're not married then?

MAN: Look . . .

LYNDA: Don't worry, Oscar had a little chat with me.

MAN: Oh yes . . . what did he say?

LYNDA: He told me not to ask any questions.

Pause.

They said at the club you always ask for the new girl – why?

Pause. The MAN *says nothing.*

They're more easily frightened, I suppose.

Pause.

Or shocked . . .

Pause.

Or sickened . . .
I suppose that's why.

Pause. The MAN *drinks.*

MAN: If you wish to leave you're quite free to do so. There's no bolt on the door.

LYNDA: Have you got a cigarette?

MAN: Of course. (*He offers an expensive cigarette.*) I thought you didn't smoke.

LYNDA: I don't. (*Her hand trembles, her voice is shaky – she inhales deeply.*)

Pause.

They said at the club, sometimes you don't mind giving a girl something . . . you know a sleeping pill . . . or something . . . so they're unconscious . . ..

The MAN *nods. Slowly* LYNDA *takes off her coat.*

Blackout.

In front of Buckingham Palace

Sound tape: traffic noises fade but are heard faintly through the scene.
Lights up. NORAH *and* STAN *in front of Buckingham Palace.* NORAH *looks through the gates.*

NORAH: We'll have beaten her home.

STAN: Who?

NORAH: Princess Margaret.

STAN: You don't know it was her.

NORAH: I used to have her photo on my desk lid – 'Margaret Rose in pink georgette'. It was her all right.

STAN: She don't live here.

NORAH: Course she does. All the royals live here.

STAN: No . . . she lives Kensington

Palace. The Queen and Prince Philip live here.

NORAH: And Charlie and Di.

STAN: Yes.

STAN *is watching* NORAH.

NORAH: I'll tell you something, Stanley . . . . It's no wonder she's always off on those Caribbean tours.

STAN: Why?

NORAH: Call that a palace, not much better than our Town Hall. I thought it'd be all shiny white with spires and little turrets, you know a proper fairy-tale palace.

STAN (*grinning*): Do you know how many windows there are?

NORAH: You what?

STAN: Windows . . . how many?

NORAH: No, but I'm sure I'm about to find out.

STAN: Six hundred and twelve windows not including 2 blocked in.

NORAH: Why are they blocked in?

STAN: I don't know.

NORAH: A ha! (*Pause.*) See that flag flying there, that means she's home. I wonder what would happen if we slipped through the gates . . . tried to pay a visit.

STAN: Couldn't do it.

NORAH: Why?

STAN: Well there's all . . . electric fences . . . and trip wires and television cameras.

NORAH: Well he managed it.

STAN: Who?

NORAH: The bloke who got in Lizzie's bedroom. They had a lovely time. Talked about the price of fish and chips.

STAN: They didn't.

NORAH: That's what I read. They're penpals now.

Pause. NORAH *shouts very loudly and aggressively.*

A piece of cod's £1.10 our way, Lizzie.

Blackout.

Wandsworth Common

Sound tape: in the distance, cars, voices, people arriving.

Lights up. MARJE *is centre-stage, at her feet the plastic bag and the butcher's meat. She paces restlessly looking out over the common.*

JOHNNY: He won't be coming.

MARJE (*turns*): Who won't be coming, Johnny?

JOHNNY: Mr Fox.

MARJE: How do you know?

JOHNNY (*he shrugs and joins her*): He wasn't here last night.

MARJE: Wasn't he?

JOHNNY: And you weren't here.

MARJE: No . . . no . . . I . . . er . . .

JOHNNY: You wasn't well.

MARJE: That's right Johnny, I wasn't well.

JOHNNY: And he wasn't here the night before – and he wasn't here the night before that . . .

MARJE: Oh he was, he was, I saw him Johnny, I . . .

She turns away and looks out over the common.

JOHNNY (*joining her; softly*): He's dead probably.

MARJE: No.

JOHNNY: Maybe if he's not out hunting. A lorry's knocked him down . . .

MARJE: No . . . no . . .

JOHNNY: Or he's trapped.

MARJE: No.

JOHNNY: Or he's been shot . . .

He makes a gun of his hand and shoots MARJE.

JOHNNY: Kk! Kk! (*He drops his 'gun'.*) You're sad. He's your friend. You bring his dinner. (*He sniggers.*) You talk to him.

MARJE *turns to him.*

I won't tell. I like it. I won't tell Jess.

MARJE *nudges the butcher's meat with her foot.*

From the house, the sound of more guests arriving.

(*Quite loudly:*) Noisy buggers. (*He laughs.*) They don't like you shouting. Scares them.

MARJE (*suddenly*): Of course, why didn't I think of it? The commotion – cars coming and going – that's why the fox isn't here. I said he should find somewhere safer.

JOHNNY: No, Mr Fox doesn't want nowhere safer. He likes watching them. (*He hisses.*) He's waiting.

MARJE: What do you mean, Johnny?

JOHNNY (*he laughs*): You're going soon.

MARJE: Am I Johnny?

JOHNNY: You're not a bad woman. You're a good woman. You've a little house with a yellow door and a number 3 – and a little dark-haired girl in a red check dress and a little boy in green trousers . . .

He laughs at MARJE's *astonished face.*

MARJE (*stunned*): How do you know all this?

JOHNNY *sniggers. Very slowly out of his inside pocket he takes out a snapshot.*

JOHNNY: I didn't steal it, I found it in this grass.

MARJE *takes it and looks at it.*

Long pause.

When you going home?

MARJE: I don't know, Johnny.

JOHNNY: Soon?

MARJE: P'raps. P'raps not. P'raps I can't go home.

JOHNNY: Can I keep it?

MARJE: Yes Johnny, you can keep it.

Blackout.

The penthouse – another room.

Lights up. LYNDA *lies unconscious on the floor. Her clothes and possessions in a jumble about her.*

Slowly she opens her eyes and for a few seconds she is absolutely still. Suddenly she remembers . . .

She tries to scramble to her knees. She is sore and stiff. Instantly she takes in her surroundings: a small square empty room . . . overhead a dazzling electric light swings gently.

Again she remembers . . . her heart starts to pound – frantically, under clothes, coat, etc. she searches for her handbag. She finds it, contents spilt, and from an inside pocket takes a small mirror. Trembling, she holds it up to her face and looks at herself.

Pause.

Her other hand, still trembling, starts to trace her features. She stops.

On the back of her neck and round her throat she discovers a red weal . . . she then sees the same weal on the wrist of the hand holding the mirror.

She starts to inspect her body . . . touching, turning, looking. There is a weal on the other wrist, also round her belly and on both ankles.

LYNDA *is terribly sore, stiff, stretched and achy!*

Her skin crawls:

BUT:

She is safe. She is in one piece.

She lets the mirror drop and her head sinks to her chest. She lets out little animal whimpers, then sobs with relief.

The sobbing stops.

Again she remembers . . . she looks about her.

A few feet away she sees a pile of crumpled, used £20 notes. She reaches out and starts to count.

LYNDA: 20 . . . 40 . . . 60 . . . 80 . . . 100 . . . 20 . . . 40 . . .

She stops. There is about £300 in £20 notes.

LYNDA *leans back on her heels.*

As she tries to make a neat pile of the £20 notes, her eye catches a small white square in amongst the money.

Pause.

Slowly LYNDA *turns it over. It is a polaroid photograph.*

LYNDA *stares at the picture taken of her by the* MAN *an hour ago in appalled and horrified fascination.*

Blackout.

Stan's bedsit

Sound tape: a clock ticking very, very softly.
Lights up. NORAH *and* STAN *are sitting by a gas fire. They share a bottle of whisky. The light is low.*

NORAH: She's never in before three so you'd expect her to sleep till, what, midday?

STAN: I suppose so.

NORAH: She never wakes till five o'clock, when she does she just starts getting ready for the night . . . then she can't seem to string two words together, dozy cow.

Pause.

And there's something else.

STAN: Go on.

NORAH: Well every night when she comes in she says she sees this fox.

STAN: So.

NORAH: Don't you think that's a bit odd. This place she goes to is by a main road.

STAN: Foxes all over London now – all over England. In 1984 at six o'clock in the morning, a fox with two cubs was seen outside Birmingham Bull Ring. It'll be like they're vermin in inner cities soon.

Pause.

NORAH: How do you know all this, Stanley?

STAN: What?

NORAH: Foxes and fossils and stuff.

STAN (*he laughs*): How does anybody know anything? I read, I listen to the radio . . . life.

Long pause. NORAH *takes in the room.*

I used to work for pest control, you you know, years ago.

NORAH: Did you?

STAN: At Smithfield Market. I'd just come to London, it was the hottest summer in fifteen years – rats were eating the carcasses . . . eating the profits, I suppose. They hired four of us to help out their regular bloke, Thompson. They had guidelines you know, do's and don'ts, but he got bored quickly did Thompson – and he had ideas of his own. One night he decided he was going to smoke out the 'filthy little bastards'. We were in the big stone cellar, Thompson blocked all the passages leading up to the warehouse except one and built a fire of sacking and straw in the corner. We waited at the bottom end of the passage. When they came running out we had to throw cat-gut nets over them and then beat at them with these wooden truncheons.

NORAH: Jesus.

STAN: Have you ever seen an animal cornered, Norah?

NORAH: No.

STAN: It was terrible. Rats when they panic, scream like – well, like children . . . we'd all been drinking. The other lads were laughing – almost hysterical, swigging back bottles of beer, red faced . . . breathless – all the time hammering down the truncheons on the . . . squirming black mass in the cat-gut net . . . . In the end there must have been one left alive. We were ready to drop with the drink and the smoke, but Thompson hadn't finished yet. He took it out of the net, jammed it against a wall with an old fireguard, he got a kettle of boiling water and poured it over the creature's scabby tail, watching it squeal and jump. Then he got matches, lit them and poked them into the thing's belly, egged another on to stub out his cigarette on the thing's greasy head, watching the fur singe and sizzle . . . with a meat hook they raked the creature's back till they drew dirty black blood . . . .

Pause.

I think after that they must have got bored. They went into the boiler room to play cards . . . .

Pause.

For a while we watched each other – the rat-catcher and the rat . . . I took the fireguard away and put my foot under the thing's backside. 'Go on,' I said, 'Shoo, shoo.' It didn't move. 'Go on,' I said, 'quick, before they come back. You won't get another chance.' Still it didn't move . . . . At last he scampered to the door. Then, suddenly, before turning into the passage, it stopped and looked at me straight in the eye, a long slow stare from clever pink eyes as if to say . . . (*He laughs, half embarrassed – half upset.*) 'Thanks. Thanks Stan.'

NORAH (*softly*): Why do you live here, Stanley?

STAN: Why? . . . I manage. I've everything I need. You haven't the same incentive when you're on your own.

NORAH: Have you no family?

STAN: A married sister back in Scotland.

NORAH: Would she visit you?

STAN: She's her own life. She'll send me a Christmas card.

NORAH: What about your wife? Do you ever hear from her?

STAN: No, not now, never.

NORAH (*standing up*): Well look, Stanley, no one'll visit you in this shit heap. Have you got a scrubbing brush?

STAN: I don't know.

NORAH: Well we'll find something and we'll give this place a real going over . . . top to bottom. You'll be able to invite the Queen here.

STAN (*getting up, panicked*): No Norah, please . . . I don't want you to do that please . . . listen, listen . . . I wanted it to be a nice evening, don't you see. I wanted . . . (*He suddenly takes her arms and makes to embrace her.*)

NORAH *remains quite still, his head buried in her. They stand for some time.*

Look Norah, I've never gone with any of the girls off the station . . . . I like them. If a girl needs her taxi-fare home, or some wally's been pestering her . . . or they just want to talk to somebody . . . they come to me.

He breaks away and moves to the drawer.

I earn a good wage . . . I don't spend it on anything . . . only food . . . the odd bottle . . . see, a week's wage. I haven't touched it . . . take it . . . I want you to have it . . . stay with me . . . please.

He embraces her, thrusting the money into her hand. NORAH *thinks. She looks at the money. She counts it. She paces around the room holding the money . . . . She looks at* STAN . . . . *Suddenly she puts the money down and goes to her bag, she takes out the book.*

NORAH: I meant to give you this before . . .. I know it's not much but . . . well . . . I've written in it.

STAN: You can't give it to me Norah, what about your . . .

NORAH (*lifts her hand*): No. I'll never make a scout.

She gets her coat, goes to the door, stops, turns, smiles.

Thanks. Thanks, Stan.

Blackout.

Wandsworth Common

Lights up. MARJE *is still by the butcher's meat. She stares out over the common.*
She hears a noise. Quickly she folds the meat into the paper and pops it into her bag . . . footsteps . . .. She turns round.

POLICE CONSTABLE: Waiting for someone?

MARJE *says nothing.*

Well? Or just catching the night air?

MARJE *says nothing.*

Can't be a bus . . . they stopped hours ago. Anyway, nearest stop's halfway up the road.

MARJE: Yes . . . I know . . . I missed the last one. I've been trying to get a taxi.

PC: Really? Where'd you phone?

MARJE *makes no answer.*

Can't be the box on the corner . . ..
It's been bollocked.

MARJE: No . . . the pub . . . I phoned
from there.

PC: The Swan? (*He looks at his watch.*)
Patient girl – you been waiting for this
taxi for . . . three hours . . . (*Pause.*)
Your friend's gone for a car ride
actually.

MARJE: My friend?

PC: Jess . . . to Hope Street Police
Station.

MARJE (*astonished*): What for?

PC: Dropping litter! What do you think –
what for.

Suddenly aggressive.

All right, turn out your pockets.

MARJE: Look, it's . . .

PC: Turn out your pockets.

MARJE *does so. In one there is about
£45.*

Dirty stuff, money (*He holds it.*) And
the other one.

*She turns out a packet of Durex with
some missing.*

All right . . . all right . . . What's your
name and address?

MARJE: It's not what you think . . .
honest . . . Look at me . . .. You don't
know me, do you? You've never seen
me before. You're right, I have been
with Jess – she's my cousin – I've been
staying with her a couple of days – she
asked me to come out with her – stops
it being so boring she says – she gave
me these to mind – but I haven't done
anything . . . I swear . . ..

Pause. He is looking at her.

PC (*softly*): Haven't done anything . . . I
can smell it on you . . .. Where's your
old man?

MARJE: What d'you mean?

PC: Send you out, did he? Earn his fag
money?

MARJE: No.

PC: Kids?

MARJE: Yes . . . but . . .

PC: Whose looking after them when

you're out on the trollope?

MARJE: My children are safe . . . I
promise.

PC: I've been called out to look at kids
from women like you . . . shut in
cupboards, half starved, playing in
their own filth, the mothers down the
boozer pouring G and T's down their
gullet.

MARJE (*breathless*): No . . . no . . . my
children are safe (*A sort of scream:*) I
promise . . . I promise.

He looks at her.

PC: You're not from round here, are
you?

MARJE: No . . . I told you . . . I'm on
holiday . . . I was visiting Jess . . . I
swear . . . I swear . . ..

*Another pause. He watches her
closely. MARJE is trembling. She
looks as if she is about to be violently
sick.*

PC (*he decides to put the money in his
pocket; sweetly*): You're lucky I'm
about to knock off – otherwise I'd
have taken you with me. I don't
happen to think you're worth ten
minutes' paperwork.

Blackout.

Marje and Norah's room

*Sound tape: the quiet ticking of a clock.
Lights up. NORAH is fully dressed.
She paces the room, occasionally
looking down onto the street. The door
clicks open and MARJE enters.*

NORAH (*almost setting about her*):
You bitch!

MARJE: I'm sorry.

NORAH: You stupid bitch. I've been
frantic about you, do you know that. I
didn't know what to do – I was just
about to call the police. I've been
making up stories past two hours
explaining why you were out in the
first place.

MARJE (*quietly*): I'm sorry.

Pause. NORAH looks at her.

NORAH: I suppose you decided to put
in a little overtime did you – eh? . . .

Being your last night. You should have told me.

MARJE: No Norah. Jess's friend didn't turn up . . . I . . . we . . . had to come back on our own.

Slight pause.

NORAH (*quietly*): I thought you'd been murdered . . .. You know that?

MARJE *is methodically getting ready for bed.*

(*Softly, watching her:*) Anyway . . . you're safe.

Pause.

Seen the fox tonight?

MARJE: No . . ..

NORAH: No elephants or giraffes?

MARJE: No.

Pause.

NORAH: I've just had Lynda in here.

MARJE: Oh yes?

NORAH: She's given me a bit of news to pass on. She's not coming back with us Saturday.

MARJE *stops what she is doing for a second.*

She's going to rent a flat – with a pal she says – still – she seems able to handle it. Good luck to her I say.

Pause. MARJE *says nothing, she gets ready for bed.*

Anyway for us that's it, all this finished. We're going home.

MARJE *says nothing.*

Did you hear me? I said we're going home . . .. We'll have a nice day tomorrow, the three of us – see a bit of London together. Lynda's taking us out for a meal tomorrow night.

MARJE: Tomorrow night?

NORAH: Yes . . . we agreed, don't you remember?

MARJE: Yes . . . yes I do.

NORAH: Our last night here together.

MARJE (*suddenly and quietly*): I won't be able to, Norah.

NORAH: Why?

MARJE: Cos I'm going out tomorrow night.

Blackout.

Lynda addresses the audience

Lights up. LYNDA *is wearing another expensive evening gown, an even more up-to-date hair-do and a professional make-up. She looks ten years older than she did at the beginning. She has the beginnings of a new voice.*

LYNDA: In the not too distant future I'd like to buy somewhere . . . a small studio flat to start with . . . somewhere nice . . . ish . . . Putney maybe or Primrose Hill and then a house outside London and a bigger luxury flat in the West End, for business purposes only. I'd like a Porsche and two holidays a year . . . Barbados and . . . Rome . . . possibly – oh, and a couple of fur coats.

At the moment most of my capital is having to be reinvested – my wardrobe, hairdressers, make-up, taxis, jewellery . . . elocution lessons . . . but if I can carry on my present earning capacity, it won't be long before I've covered overheads and I hit *pure profit*.

I'm a hard worker. I'm not supporting a habit, or . . . a pimp. I won't get pregnant.

In years to come I'll register myself as a small business . . . a little office somewhere . . . find a catchy title . . . 'Escort Elite' . . . get a few names and addresses on my books, boys as well as girls . . . only the best types . . . you know, educated, and well spoken . . . (*Ecstatically:*) I'll pay tax.

Don't get me wrong. I've every sympathy with women like Norah and Marje, but I can't help thinking they bring a lot on themselves. I dragged myself up from the gutter – why can't they?

Wandsworth Common

Lights up. MARJE *waiting. Slow footsteps. The* POLICE CONSTABLE *appears.*

PC: You almost took me in, do you know that?

MARJE *says nothing.*

All that bilge about only holding the sausage skins for her, up from the north . . . keeping her company . . . minding her fivers . . . I must be going soft.

MARJE *says nothing.*

It was the look in your eye what did it.

MARJE: I . . . don't understand.

He bars the way.

PC: I've eye-balled all sorts of tarts from rich bitches to your out and out scrubbers working a rough patch . . . but I never seen that look on a tart. Almost fooled me that did.

MARJE (*attempts to go*): . . . I've done nothing wrong . . . it's late and I must go, really.

PC: You're going nowhere, girl. You and me going to enjoy the night air.

They both stand side by side for some time. He looks out.

Nice houses . . . this end . . . nice houses . . . nice cars . . . nice gardens . . . nice people.
   We took a lot of stick when you lot moved in you know.
   Police Commissioner's daughter lives here somewhere. (*He gestures vaguely.*)
   Doesn't want her poodle out walkies coming across some bint legs akimbo . . . and the kids, they ask questions . . . (*As a posh little girl:*) 'Mummy, who's that funny lady standing at the bottom of the garden?' . . . 'Mummy, that lady's on the floor fighting with a man again.'
   It's the type scrubbers like you attract that's particularly antisocial. The way I see it you're like a jam pot and it's not too long before there's lots of dirty little flies buzzing round you . . . winos . . . loonies . . . blacks . . . cripples . . . the odd jack the lad not getting it at home. These types leave a mess behind them – that's when they send for us you see . . . clean up after you . . . so they don't dirty their 'lilly-whites'.

MARJE: You can't keep me here against my will. You've no proof against me.

PC: The look in your eye interests me.

Blackout.

Wandsworth Common

Lights up. A tight spot on MARJE's *face. She whispers.*

MARJE: This side of the common. The near side. By the wide road and the big houses with gardens that lean over in the commonland and make fingers and disappear.
   Some have high walls ancient with ivy . . . some want you to look in – and stand in the shining, only for a minute mind and see . . . palaces.
   Sometimes, not often now, they come out. Their voices slice the night like axes. They jingle. They wear dead animals.
   But then came the foxes of the common who dug lairs in the gardens of the big houses and who at dusk pressed their noses against the golden glass and licked their lips.
   So the shining people sent for the men with traps and the men with guns and the men with poison and the foxes howled as they lay crushed and tortured sometimes for days . . . and even the shining people said the howling was indeed terrible to hear.
   But one fox escaped the shooting, learned to spit out the poison and on the terrible steel traps, started to sharpen her teeth.

Blackout.

Wandsworth Common

Blackout.
   Suddenly a dreadful howl.
   Lights up. MARJE *has pushed the* PC *from her. He is half naked. He tries to cover himself.*

PC (*alarmed at the noise*): Stupid cunt!

MARJE: No!

PC (*fumbling with his clothing*): You silly fucking bitch. Shut your mouth, do you hear me?

   MARJE *looks at him. She is trembling violently.*

PC (*still fumbling*): I've got your

number. You're not a regular prostitute. Think I'd be here if you was a filthy scrubber. You're a silly cow down on her luck, thinking she can get the rent money with it. And don't tell me I'm the only one who's had a freeby . . . You're a sitting duck, lady . . . I'm surprised they ain't queuing half way to Streatham.

MARJE (*very quietly*): You're right . . . almost right. I was . . . well . . . an ordinary woman. I lived in a little house with my husband and two nice children in a little town and we had jobs and a future – but gradually they took it all away from us. First they took my husband's job. With that, because of the sort of man he is, went his dignity . . .. Gradually he turned into a violent man who raised his hands against his children and against me – and then of course they took his self-respect – and with his job went all the jobs and with them, my children's future. Finally, they even took my paltry little job and my wage. Do you know what I did? It's funny really. I worked in a meat-pudding factory (*She laughs.*) So then we had to beg for every last crumb – for food – for heating – for light – for air – and we realised we were worth nothing, and by then, because we were worthless they wanted us to shut our doors, stay quiet, stay inside, so no one could see us, or hear us, so they could forget us. But I did something extraordinary – I came out and I came here. I still had something – one last thing they couldn't take from me – they hadn't skinned me yet! And every time a man brutalised and defiled me I thought only with this, only with my pain and humiliation, only with my skin can I buy survival for my family . . . only with this.
And I am still selling it – my skin, but I am selling it . . . not giving it away, do you hear? If you want me you will pay just like everyone else.

PC (*quietly*): I should have known shouldn't I . . . that look in your eye . . .. You're bonkers, aren't you, eh? A real little loony.

MARJE: More, because yesterday you stole from me.

PC: Me . . . pay? Don't you know you have to be nice to me? Don't you know what trouble I could make for you? . . . for your family . . . take you into the station now . . . Don't you realise?

MARJE: Do it then.

PC: You what?

MARJE: Take me to the station. Come on. Let's go together – and I will tell them what you tried to do to me.

PC: You will, will you? You'll tell them, will you? Do you think anybody will listen to a word you say? Do you think anyone's interested in you? Do you think anybody'd believe your word against mine? Nobody cares for the likes of you. You're a boil on the backside of this country, lady, filth like you.

MARJE: Let's put it to the test.

PC: What?

MARJE: I will tell them why I was here tonight. I will tell them everything . . .. That I was an ordinary person, that I had children to feed and clothe and I will tell them . . . you stole from me and that you defiled me . . . and they will believe me, do you hear? They will all believe me. Because I am speaking the truth.

He looks at her amazed . . . a little unnerved . . . he starts laughing uneasily.

PC: It's going to be fun and games, I can see that. Old Sarge'll never have had such a laugh in years.

He takes out his transistor.

(*Viciously:*) All right, lady, lead the way – go on – keep to the path – where I can see.

MARJE *starts out over the common. He is about to speak into his radio when he notices something . . . to his left . . . then to his right . . . then behind . . . then in front. He looks all around him. He is alarmed. He drops the radio.*

Jesus . . .

Blackout.

King's Cross Station

Sound tape: busy station.
Lights up very slowly. MARJE,
CARESS, NORAH *and* LYNDA *stand
in a line facing the audience.* NORAH
and MARJE *have their suitcases. When
the lights are at half brightness the
station noise stops and* MARJE *speaks.
Through her speech the light on her
increases.*

MARJE: I walked back along the stone
path, this way, with the lampposts
behind me. I knew I would see right
across the commonland – across from
the railway bridge to the gardens of
the big houses. It was here I saw the
fox.
    At first I couldn't make out what
was happening. It appeared to be
jumping up and down, each time
higher than the time before, twisting its
body first one way then another, quite
graceful, as if to its own pan-pipe. It
was then that I realised that the fox
was dancing – that there, close to the
wide road and the big houses with the
great golden glass . . . the little fox
was dancing, throwing its body again
and again into the misty air.

Thatcher's Women

I was watching a late-night discussion programme. A spokeswoman from something called 'The English Collective of Prostitutes' was talking about the harassment of prostitutes in King's Cross. The situation was being made worse, she said, by the appearance, on the streets, of ordinary women, 'housewives' from the north-east, north-west, Midlands and Scotland, coming down to London to work as prostitutes for short periods in order to pay the rent, feed and clothe their children. They were spilling out of the trains onto the station platforms, quite literally, in their thousands!

The tabloid press were calling it 'a phenomena'. The prostitutes of King's Cross had given them their own name. They called them 'Thatcher's women'.

On the six o'clock news earlier that week another phrase had caught my attention. Michael Heseltine, talking about his vision of the future, had spoken of 'caring capitalism'.

After leaving school and before going to RADA, I had worked in a meat-pudding factory in Manchester. Many of the husbands of the women who worked there would be unemployed now, victims of the massive redundancies that hit Trafford Park. What of the fate of the factory itself? Was it possible that these women might be forced to board the trains south?

I had always wanted to write but I'd been putting it off (writing was something I was going to do when I was older!). However, in this instance I did actually sit down, and very quickly wrote a first half – then went to act in a play in Liverpool and forgot about it.

When I read the rough first half some while later, I was disappointed – it seemed thin and a bit ploddy. I kept hearing that woman on the television talk about 'ordinary women'. Looking at what I'd written, I felt that as the situation the women found themselves in became more extraordinary so too should the play. I decided I wanted to write a play that started out being very naturalistic, but changed.

My central character was already very real to me. I had worked with an actress called Marjorie Yates. I think she is a wonderful and unique actress because she combines exactly these qualities. The ordinary and the extraordinary. A version of Marjorie Yates was becoming Marje.

By this time I was touring in a play. I arrived back at my flat in Streatham, South London at four o'clock one morning. It is a stone's throw from a busy main road and a complex of high rise flats and office buildings. Getting out of the car, walking up the path, I was aware of something in the road . . . smaller than a dog, larger than a cat, watching me.

There, under a lamppost, close to the cars and the houses and the gardens, frozen, absolutely still, was a fox. I'd never seen a live one before – and we were staring at each other; then, suddenly, it turned into one of the gardens and disappeared.

I was thrilled, excited, horrified. I felt I had seen something very secret – and dangerous! And I had the second half of my play.

Pip Broughton, Director of Paines Plough, was one of the first people to read my play. I was very lucky because she commissioned me to write a second draft.

Working with Pip on *Thatcher's Women* was an utterly joyful experience for me. We discussed which areas of the play needed developing and which were over-developed. We cut out a good deal of the first half set in Manchester which looked at the circumstances that sent the women to London (deciding that a lot of this could be taken for granted) and concentrated on what happened to them once they were there. Pip wanted me to find more animal imagery in the story (I wrote Marje's Belle Vue speech and Stan's rat speech). I developed the Norah-Stan relationship; and as Marje's story shifted on to another level in the second half, so also did Lynda's (as Marje finds her voice in the second half of the play, Lynda loses hers, until the capitalist speech when she finally addresses the audience). I also cut out Gladys, an OAP who appeared in the first draft, making the play tighter and more focused. I enjoyed the process of rewriting so much.

Pip decided on a rehearsed reading in front of an audience at the Young Vic. The play worked better than I had hoped. After the usual delays and setbacks, it was finally decided *Thatcher's Women* would run for a month at the Tricycle Theatre (prior to touring).

I helped cast (which was the worst bit), and sat in on the first two weeks of rehearsal. I decided to accept an acting job for the last two weeks of rehearsal and into the run at the Tricycle. because I was frightened my being there all the time might be inhibiting; and anyway it's a sort of 'act of faith' – after a while you just have to hand it over lock, stock and barrel.

I also trusted Pip and, by now, the actors, who were very special; and wonderful in their commitment to the play.

I had had long discussions with Pip about how I thought it should look and feel, i.e. sensual, emotional, intimate . . . female, etc. Ellen Cairns created a design that painted the stage with colour and shapes and 'felt' extraordinary.

The play opened on 12 March 1987.

I'm actually writing this on 11 April 1988. I'm a child of the Welfare State. I grew up in the sixties and seventies. If you were a single parent; if you were old or young, disabled, mentally handicapped or with a mental illness, unemployed, low paid, if you were struggling and in difficulty, there was the possibility out there . . . somewhere . . . of help.

I have a baby daughter. She will be growing up in the 1990s. In the year 2000 she'll be thirteen. They say, don't they, you judge a society by how it treats its most vulnerable. I'd better enroll her in a pre-school accountancy course quick! Perhaps I could get her modelling bibs, or nappies . . . baby food. She'd better learn to stand on her own two feet. She'd better not have a run of bad luck. She'd better not be poor or, worse still, sick, because unless the tide turns I can't see that there's going to be any help for her.

Thatcher's Women is my first full-length play. I learnt an enormous amount. I'd like to thank Pip Broughton, the actors, Paines Plough and the Tricycle Theatre.

Kay Adshead trained as an actress at RADA. She has played leading roles in theatre, film and television, notably Cathy in the BBC classic series *Wuthering Heights*, Beryl Stapelton in *Hound of the Baskervilles*, Lynda in Mike Leigh's film *The Kiss of Death* and Sue McKenna in Film on Four's *Acceptable Levels*. She was Moll Gromer in *Thee and Me* at the National Theatre, Betty in Richard Eyre's *Touched* at the Old Vic, Tanzi in *Trafford Tanzi* at the Mermaid, and Constanze in the National Theatre's tour of *Amadeus*.

Thatcher's Women is her first full-length play. She is currently working on *Bacillus*, a play set in 1999, commissioned by the Royal Court.

ADULT CHILD/DEAD CHILD

Claire Dowie

Adult Child/Dead Child was first presented at the Finborough Theatre Club, London, on 5 June 1987, before touring nationally.

Performed by Claire Dowie
Directed by Colin Watkeys

When you are a child
& you don't get any love, when there is
   no love
when you get this feeling that you can't
   explain
this feeling that's inside you but you can't
   explain
you don't know what it is, you can't say
   it's lack of love
because you don't have those words
you only have the feeling but you don't
   have those words
those words that say nobody loves me, I
   am unloved
all you have is the feeling
& the feeling is an empty feeling, a hole
   in your stomach
you feel this hole in your stomach that
   you can't explain
because you don't have the words, only
   the feeling, the empty feeling
& the feeling hurts, you feel hurt because
   you can't explain
you feel hurt & frustrated that there is
   no love
& you can't explain, you feel trapped in
   your feelings
trapped in your feelings of hurt &
   frustration & lack of love
lack of love that makes you hit out

Clean house, tidy house
spotless
nothing out of place
except me
can't seem to please them
can't win for losing
my mother despaired of me
I despaired of me.
My sister was an angel
never put a foot wrong
always clean, always tidy
a perfect child, a joy to behold.

A spotless, squeaky clean hall floor
muddy shoes tramped from school
footprints – my mother's anger
my mother's annoyance
I would've walked on the ceiling if I
   could
like spiderman
but I expect the ceiling was squeaky
   clean too.

My father was an actor
professional pretender
pretended to be a father
pretended to have feelings
pretended enthusiasm
demanded perfection
demanded perfection
100% do it right, do it the best
be brainy, be sporty, be talented, be
   good
academic athlete
well mannered, polite, know it all, do it
   all
100% do it right, do it the best
I cried, I would cry
I would cry & I failed
always failed
for my professional pretending father
& his daughter, the apple of his eye
who could do no wrong.

I remember being in the garden of our
old house, I was about six or seven &
there were friends of my parents visiting.
I can't remember now who, but
somebody gave me a cowboy & indian
set. This was a cowboy hat & gun &
holster & a tin star with the word
'sheriff' on it & an indian feather thing
with a band on it for a hat & a
tomahawk & my dad said let's play with
it & first he was the cowboy & I was the
indian & everybody was watching & I
ran at him with my tomahawk but he
shot me so I lost & then we changed
round & I was the cowboy & my dad
was the indian but before I could shoot
him he threw the tomahawk & it hit my
head & he said it was Custer's last stand
& everybody laughed (I thought he said
'custard' & I didn't understand) & he
said I was hopeless because I died twice
& I didn't want to play with my cowboy
& indian set anymore but later on that
night I decided to be the indian & sneak
up on him quietly but when I sneaked
into their bedroom & jumped on him
with my tomahawk he woke up. Didn't
act like a cowboy, acted like an angry
father.

Clumsy, I was clumsy
I was a clumsy child
knocked things, broke things
a clumsy child
always falling over, breaking things
trying to avoid running into things
swerving round things
trying not to be clumsy
trying to walk through the gap in the
   doorframe

instead of into the doorframe
trying to stop my body moving before it
    was too late
it was always too late
I was a clumsy child
clumsy

Never a day would go by that I wasn't
walking into things, tripping up, knocking
things over & banging & crashing my
way about the house. It worried me. It
drove my parents crazy.
Fidgeting was another habit I couldn't
seem to shake off which annoyed my
parents intensely. Once my dad got so
mad about it that he tied me down
rigidly to a chair for a while. Strangely it
didn't stop me feeling fidgety, just
stopped me being fidgety.

& the cupboard, the cupboard under the
    stairs
I wasn't abused
I was never what you'd call an abused
    child
not abused
not by any stretch of the imagination
but there was the cupboard, the
    cupboard under the stairs
dark, silent, claustrophobic
nothing to do, nothing to say, nothing to
    be but lifeless, invisible
nowhere, nothing
sitting in the cupboard till I 'learn to
    behave myself & show some respect'
in the cupboard under the stairs
& eye for eye & tooth for tooth
    punishments
my parents were great believers in
'see how you like it'
eye for eye & tooth for tooth
    punishments
I was never abused
not what you'd call an abused child
not abused
everything I got I deserved
except the cupboard, the cupboard under
    the stairs
I never locked anyone in a cupboard
but my parents did.

I remember when we moved I was about
eight & my sister & I went to stay with
friends of my parents for a week,
probably to get us out of the way while
the moving was sorted out. The friends
of my parents had a son called Andrew,
who was I think, a couple of years older

& when nobody was around he'd punch
me & pinch me. His parents wouldn't
believe me.
Before we moved I asked my mom where
London was & she said it was a hundred
miles away, I was very worried about it
staying with these friends of my parents
& Andrew. A hundred miles is a long
way to run when you're eight.
I remember being very relieved that
there wasn't a cupboard under the stairs
at our new flat in London. Then I found
out there was a broom cupboard which
was much smaller.

You want to hit out because of this lack
    of love that you can't explain
so you hit out because of this lack of love
you hit out at the people around you
hit out at the people, the adults around
    you
the adults around you when you are a
    child
because when you are a child the adults
    have the power
the adults have the power & they know
    everything
they know everything so they know your
    feelings
adults understand feelings, they can
    explain your feelings
because adults have the power to explain
    feelings
to know what you are feeling so you hit
    out
you hit out because they won't help you
    with your feelings
because you have these feelings but they
    won't help
they won't help you with these empty
    feelings
these empty feelings that hurt but you
    can't explain
this hurt & frustration because you can't
    explain
so you stop trusting the adults

My invisible friend
a voice in my head
I could talk to her
I played with her
we understood each other
she was reliable.
She came I think when I was four or five
or maybe earlier, who knows
but by the age of seven
she was with me always

chattering away, making jokes
telling stories
poking fun at family & visitors
making me laugh at all times
at lonely times, good times
boring times, embarrassing times
& awkward times
when I giggled
& my parents wondered about me
& punished me for being bad mannered
impolite or stupid

I didn't give my invisible friend a name
till I was eight. I don't know why, I don't
know why she was a girl either, she just
was & she was just nameless till we
moved to London. I hated London. I
hated the school I had to go to because
they beat me up because I talked funny,
I hated the flat we'd moved to because it
was smaller & so was the cupboard, & I
hated the street where we lived because
it was snobby & stuck up but I loved my
lady. My lady lived down the road from
us & she was always pottering around
her front garden with her dog Benji,
stopping to chat to people as they passed
including me. She called me 'scallywag'
& she spoke nicely to me. She
made me feel special & I loved her even
though I didn't know what 'scallywag'
meant, but I knew it was a nice name
because she also called Benji a scallywag
& I could tell that she loved him very
much & never hurt or ignored him even
though she also called him a monster &
a horror & a terror. I would spend hours
sometimes going up & down the road so
that my lady could say 'hello scallywag'
& I could say 'hello' back. Sometimes
she would say 'off on your travels
scallywag?' when I passed & sometimes
she would say 'jaunting again
scallywag?'. One thing she never asked
was why I was always walking up &
down the road.
One day I was coming down the road
trying to make up my mind if I was
travelling or jaunting when I passed my
next-door neighbours, the Bannermans.
They had been talking to my lady & as I
passed I overheard Mr Bannerman say
'she's a stupid old cow isn't she'.

Well I was angry, I was angry
I was so upset & too confused
to look her in the eye & say hello
I was just so angry

I had to run, had to pass her
couldn't stop, couldn't smile
I just ran, just so angry
what he said, how could he say that
about my lady, my lovely lady
just got so upset, so angry
couldn't say hello, couldn't pretend to
    smile
just had to run
just had to run to my house & sit in My
    Place
just had to run & sit in My Place.

(My Place incidentally was the narrow
gap between the shed & the fence where
nobody thought of looking.)

& I sat in My Place & my invisible friend
sat in My Place & we fumed about the
Bannermans & my invisible friend said
'Something's got to be done'. I agreed
but didn't know what, so we sat in
silence for a while till my invisible friend
decided that if they were going down the
road (which they were) it must mean that
they were going out, & if they were going
out (which they must have been) then
that means that they're not in & if they
are not in (which they weren't) then we
should put a brick through their window
& since I can't because I'm invisible
(which she was) then you'll have to do it
(which I didn't want to do because it was
wrong & I was scared). This was when
we started arguing & my invisible friend
told me that if I didn't put a brick
through the Bannerman's window she
was going to go away & never speak to
me again.

My invisible friend
the voice in my head
I talked to her
I played with her
we understood each other
she was reliable.
She threatened to leave
she said she'd go
I was only eight
I didn't realise what was happening
what was beginning
I was just scared at that point
of loneliness
of immediate loneliness
I didn't realise what was happening
what was beginning
what would happen later on

but that was the starting point
that's when I began to lose control.

Blackmail, threats, treachery & hatred.

So of course finally I had to agree &
finally I did put a brick through the
Bannermans' window after making sure
first that my father was still out & my
mother was engrossed in the hoovering.
So I threw a brick through the
Bannermans' window. After I'd thrown
the brick & heard the glass shatter I ran
back to My Place & waited five or ten
minutes to see if the sky would fall in or
(worse) my father would appear. It
didn't & he didn't & nobody started
shouting & nothing happened &
everything was still all right even though
I'd done a wrong thing. & not only that
but I also felt triumphant & happy &
giggled uncontrollably for ages. My
invisible friend giggled uncontrollably too
& then she told me she had loads of
ideas that would be really funny to do in
the future. I wasn't so sure & asked her
if they were wrong things but she just
giggled some more & said 'wait & see'.
So it was then that I decided that my
invisible friend was really, when all was
said & done, a monster & a horror & a
terror & I called her Benji.

You stop trusting the adults because they
    have the power
they have the power but won't help
so you don't trust them, they are against
    you
they are against you because they won't
    help
& they have the power to help but they
    won't
so you don't trust them, because they
    won't help
so you start to hate them because you
    don't trust them
you start to hate them because they
    won't help
you hit out because you hate them

My parents had always known about my
invisible friend. She sat next to me at the
dinner table (& she didn't like cabbage
either). Occasionally, through me she'd
ask them a question, they'd answer. By
the time I was eight & had called her
Benji, they were telling me I was too old

for imaginary friends. Stupid. Benji was
still there, I could hear her, I could feel
her, she talked to me, I played with her.
& we did things together.

Little things, easy things
so what if that ornament got broken
it just sat there anyway
didn't do anything
& if they asked me well
I dunno, wasn't me
I was nowhere near it
& what money?
I don't know anything about any money
& so what if my sister lost her charm
    bracelet
it was a horrible charm bracelet
it rattled
anyway I don't know
maybe she just dropped it somewhere
maybe it just fell off
I don't know.

We got away with it for a long time,
mostly because Benji was a good liar &
would tell me what to say if anyone
asked. One day my mother said:

You just broke that picture
what?
you just broke it
no I didn't
yes you did I saw you
no it was an accident
no it wasn't I saw you
it was an accident
you picked it up & threw it on the floor
no I didn't
I just saw you
it was an accident
I saw you
Benji did it
oh don't be so stupid
she did
will you stop that Benji stuff, it was you
no it was Benji
look it was you, now just stop it, you're
    too old for all that rubbish
but she did.

I was too old for imaginary friends but
Benji was still with me, even so I got the
blame, & the cupboard for telling lies.

& so it started.

Slowly
a little bit at a time

a little more each day
moving away further & further
making it more difficult to understand
  each other
making it more difficult to try
they were far away from me over that
  side; parents, sister, teachers
everybody.
Benji & I were on this side
My lady I could still reach, still connect
  with, she was in the middle.
But then she left.

I knew she was leaving she told me
I was sad about it but didn't show it
Just wanted to buy her a leaving present
a remembrance of me
a dog
an ornament of a dog
but it was expensive, couldn't afford it
had no money
couldn't afford anything with no money.
Benji got hold of some money
we bought the dog the day before
give it to her in the morning
we said, we thought
I got up early especially
I was washed, I was dressed
I didn't want any breakfast

But then my mother starts.
She's going on & on about some money
missing from her purse, she wants to
know, my dad joins in, my sister sits
there all innocent & perfect, they're on
at me, on at me, I don't want to know,
not now, I just want to go up the road &
give my lady her present, I can't be
bothered with this money business right
now, when I get home from school fair
enough, but not now, its getting on my
nerves all their questions, accusations,
fingers pointing in my face, Benji's
getting annoyed, Benji's getting angry, I
can feel her, not now, I don't want this
kind of thing now, I just want to go up
the road & give my lady her present,
she's leaving, I've got to give it to her
before she leaves, before its too late. My
mother going on & on, my father poking
his nose in, my sister sitting there smug
& silent, Benji goes mad, I can't control
her, I've lost control of her, can't control
her outburst, its not helping, my parents
have really got something to say now,
really got it in for me now, & I don't
want this, I just want to go up the road
before she leaves.

I didn't know her name, I never did
know her name. I don't think she knew
mine either, she just called me
'scallywag' & I was happy with that. I
couldn't explain it to my parents, I
couldn't tell them about her, never had,
she was my secret, they didn't know & if
I'd tried to explain they would probably
have thought I was making it up as an
excuse or something, a lie. & they
certainly wouldn't have believed that it
was Benji who took the money.
My dad drove me to school that morning
because I was late with all the arguing. I
didn't bother listening to his lecture, just
looked out of the window with my hand
in my pocket holding the ornament. I
couldn't see too much of my lady's house
as we passed it because of the big
Pickford's van in front but I caught a
glimpse of Benji pissing against the tree
in the garden. When I came home from
school the house was empty, my lady was
gone, I'd missed her. I didn't know what
to do with the ornament so I posted it
through her letterbox, I heard it break as
it hit the floor (no carpets). It didn't
matter, I had no use for it anyway.

You build a wall of anger & mistrust &
  hatred
& you build a wall because they wouldn't
  help you
& you hate these adults because they
  made you build a wall
they made you build a wall of hatred
  because they wouldn't help
& you hit out because they made you
  build the wall
you hit out in hatred because of the wall
  that you built
& the wall gets stronger because your
  hatred grows
& your hatred grows as awareness comes

Further & further away, no
understanding, no communication. Just
me & Benji in our own little world & all
the rest of them in theirs. Miles apart &
no bridges. The only time our worlds
collided was when Benji did something
wrong & I got the blame for it.
At school I had to see a child
psychologist. What an idiot.
Benji would swear. It wouldn't have
been so bad if it was just swearing, if it

was just swearing, if Benji just swore, it
wouldn't have been so bad. But it
wasn't, wasn't just swearing, Benji stole.
She stole. She stole money, from my
parents, from my school mates, from
everybody, she needn't, she didn't have
to, she didn't need it. & shoplifting,
shop-lifting & stealing things, silly things,
she didn't need them, she stole a toy car
once, she didn't need it, she didn't even
like it, she threw it away later, &
travelling, going off jaunting, playing
truant from school, not turning up just
jaunting off anywhere, travelling around.
& she shouted, & she shouted at people
& threw things, she'd go mad & shout at
people & throw things, tantrums, she had
tantrums & shouted at people & threw
things, threw things at the wall, all over
the room, threw the furniture & the
ornaments at the walls & all over the
room & at people, she threw things at
people & shouted at them & swore at
them, she swore, it wouldn't have been
so bad if she just swore but she didn't.
She was wild, uncontrollable. She
thought it was funny, I didn't, I never
wanted to get into trouble, I never did
want to get into all that trouble. They
wouldn't believe me that it was Benji so
I stopped telling them. It was just trouble
all the time, trouble all the time & Benji
was laughing. I couldn't control her, I
couldn't stop her. She scared me.
Benji loved words like outlaw, hooligan,
gangster, delinquent, vandal – she
thought they sounded good, romantic,
exciting.

Mr Kent
he was a woodwork teacher
& a bastard
by now I was thirteen
& hated by everybody
including Mr Kent
it was about a year since my lady left
& I'd been at war with Benji on & off
    since then
I was at war with Benji
& everybody was at war with me.
I was making a toast rack in woodwork
Mr Kent said I was an idiot
I was proud of my toast rack
Mr Kent said it was crap
Mr Kent said I was useless
Mr Kent said I was a worthless specimen
    of a human being
Mr Kent went on & on & on

till Benji jumped out
& threw a hammer at him.

Everybody was further away from me.
Everybody & everything way off in the
distance. I couldn't connect at all, not at
all, I didn't even know how to try, I
didn't know anything because I was on
this side, way over here & Benji, Benji
was in the middle now, in control. Benji
was in control of everything now, & I
hated her.

Luckily it missed
but I was sent to the headmaster
he started shouting
but I couldn't understand
couldn't make sense of it
Benji understood cus she was answering
    him
but I don't know what she said
because I couldn't understand
couldn't make sense of it
I doubt if she was apologising though.
I'm aware that he's phoning my parents
I don't understand what's happening
I'm aware that they're out
because he doesn't talk to the telephone

He says they will be contacted
& asked to come to the school
it's filtering through but it makes no
    sense
Benji understands cus she's smirking
I am aware of that.
I get sent home
I go home
in the evening they get the phone call
they are asked to go but they don't know
    why
just that they have to discuss me
I am to be discussed
they have to go to discuss me
they asked me why
I didn't answer
I said I don't know
because I didn't, really
it doesn't make sense
but I am aware
that they are looking at me
with hatred

All night, it was a long night, it was
black & then it was dawn. All night, a
long night, I am awake, or sort of
awake, or something, I'm not sure, I
don't know what's happening with me,
Benji doesn't stop talking, doesn't stop

telling me that my dad's going to kill me
when he finds out, all night, I can't
sleep, Benji won't shut up, I don't know
what's happening to me, I can't seem to
sort anything out, I can't seem to
understand anything, all night, & Benji
keeps telling me, keeps talking, an eye
for an eye, he's going to kill you when he
finds out, all night, a long night, such a
long night, & Benji telling me over &
over, remember when you kicked your
sister how he kicked you, remember
when you threw stones at those boys how
he threw stones at you, an eye for an
eye, tooth for tooth, remember when you
broke his record, he broke your toys,
remember when you broke his wing
mirror he broke your bike, eye for eye,
tooth for tooth, remember when you
smashed the radio he smashed your
record player, remember when you
wrecked the living room he wrecked your
bedroom, all night, all night, & I never
did those things, I never did, Benji did
them, it was Benji, I don't know what's
happening, I don't, & the cupboard
after, the cupboard after, the cupboard,
cupboard, he's going to kill you, see how
you like it, remember the ashtray, the
ashtray, you threw it at him, it was the
same, you threw the ashtray, remember
it didn't hit him did it, it didn't hit him,
but he was going to hit you wasn't he, he
was, you could tell couldn't you, ah yes,
you could tell, he was going to hit you
with the ashtray, wasn't he, he was, she
stopped him, remember she stopped him,
she said don't, & she stopped him, but
he was going to, he was going to hit you
with the ashtray remember he was, he
would have if she hadn't stopped him, &
now look what you've done, I didn't do
anything, it was you, you threw it, it was
you, you did it, but they won't believe
you will they, they never do, they never
did, you threw the hammer, what's he
going to do, think about it, what's he
going to do, I can't think, shut up please,
leave me alone, eye for eye, tooth for
tooth, you threw the hammer, what's he
going to do, think about it, he's going to
kill you when he finds out, he's going to
kill you, eye for eye, & tooth for tooth,
remember & then the cupboard, what're
you going to do, what are you going to
do now, remember, remember the
ashtray, he's going to kill you now that's
what, unless you kill him first, unless you
do it first, to save yourself, to defend
yourself, eye for eye, defend yourself,
tooth for tooth, when he finds out, what
are you going to do, you're going to die
that's what you'll do, when he finds out,
you'll die, he'll kill you, he'll kill you
when he finds out, eye for eye, tooth for
tooth, you've got to defend yourself,
you've got to find the hammer first,
before he finds out, you've got to find
the hammer, you've got to defend
yourself, eye for eye, tooth for tooth, &
then the cupboard, & then the cupboard,
find the hammer, eye for eye he's going
to kill you when he finds out, remember,
remember the ashtray, remember, all
night, all night, it was a long night, all
night & I don't know, I can't understand
any more, I don't know what's
happening to me & Benji won't shut up,
& I do remember the ashtray, I do
remember that, I do remember that she
stopped him, & I don't know anymore, I
can't understand, I can't think right, I
don't know & it's all night, all night, it's
black & then it's dawn & then I'm there
in their bedroom with the hammer & I
don't know how, I don't know, I don't
understand & then I hit him with it, I hit
him, I don't understand, I don't know
what's happening, & then he wakes up,
he wakes up.

He woke up
I hit him
I caught him on the head & he woke up
it woke him, it hurt.
I dropped the hammer
I turned & left the room
left the flat
I went travelling
Benji took me travelling
we went miles
I don't know where we went
we just travelled
& the police picked me up
my mom fetched me
after the police had phoned
it was late, they found me wandering
I was just travelling, just jaunting
Benji took me, we just went
& then my mom picked me up
collected me from the police station
& brought me home
& she stopped at a shop & bought me a
　Mars bar & a packet of crisps
& I knew then that I'd be in the
　cupboard all night

& it didn't matter.

You start to hit out in hatred because
   they have the power
you hit out in hatred but you still can't
   explain
you still can't explain because they've
   never helped you
they had the power but they never
   helped you
so you hit out in hatred but you can't
   explain
you can't explain this hatred, this feeling
   of hatred
this feeling of hatred & mistrust for these
   people
these adults who had the power but
   wouldn't help
so you build a wall around you

Lunatic
lunacy
loony
mad
insane
I didn't know anything about
   psychiatrists
or mental health
or anything
except what I'd heard
& read
& watched on television

Deranged
psychopath
psycho

& then I had to see one
had to see a psychiatrist
not for hitting my dad
but for hitting
myself
loony
mad
crazy.

It was mad. Totally out of hand. I didn't
know what else to do really. I was under
virtual house arrest at home, it was
barmy. I'd been suspended from school
for two weeks because Mr Kent & the
headmaster couldn't take a joke, well all
right, it wasn't funny, no, it was very
dangerous, but it had missed & he had
asked for it. Anyway my parents decided
to keep an eye on me. I think basically

they were scared stiff of me, I don't
blame them really I was pretty loopy
around that time, but if anything's
guaranteed to drive you mad it's having
your parents & sister tiptoeing around
the place, glancing sidelong at you all the
time, locking your bedroom door every
night, not saying anything about
anything, & then trying to pretend that
nothing's happened & everything's hunky
dory. We should have talked about it,
somebody should have said something,
done something, anything, I was feeling
terrible about it, I didn't know what to
do, how to apologise. Nothing happened,
nobody said a word, nobody did a thing,
they just watched me, kept me in the
house, hardly spoke a word to me &
watched me, & locked my bedroom door
at night. What could I do, how could I
explain, it was mad, it was driving me
mad. & Benji. I had to put up with
Benji. I could feel her bubbling under all
the time with all the tension, I knew she
was going to explode soon if something
didn't happen. She couldn't bear it, I
couldn't bear it, we couldn't go on like
that, with my parents tiptoeing around
not knowing what to do with me, being
scared of me, watching me, my dad
sitting there with a big purple bruise on
his head as if nothing had happened, &
Benji inside me, bubbling, beginning to
get restless, starting to rage about the
atmosphere. Couldn't go on like that,
somebody had to do something,
somebody had to make a move, stop the
tension, do something before Benji did.
So I did, I did something, I did what they
wanted to do, did what my dad should
have done, get it over with, get it out of
the way, clear the air, make amends,
even the score, so, eye for eye, tooth for
tooth, I hit myself with the hammer.
That made something happen, made
somebody say something, do something.
It did. They sent me to a psychiatrist.

Lunatic.

I was scared. I was scared because the
psychiatrist was asking me questions,
talking to me & making complete sense
to me. I was scared because I could
understand what he was getting at, what
he was asking, things like 'do you ever
feel out of control?' & 'do you feel that
your parents don't understand you?'. I

couldn't answer because Benji told me
not to, Benji didn't have to tell me not
to, I wasn't going to answer anyway, I
wasn't going to because I was scared stiff
of this psychiatrist finding out I was
loony. & he would have too because he
made sense, his questions made sense to
me. I was terrified.

The Snake Pit.
I saw a film once called the Snake Pit
it was a film about a loony bin
it was horrible, awful, scary
I was scared to go to the Snake Pit
I thought I'd get sent to the Snake Pit
get put in the Snake Pit
in the loony bin
couldn't answer his questions or he'd
    know
he'd know I was loony
& I'd get put in the loony bin
in the Snake Pit.

& he asked about the hammer, & I got
scared then. He said first you tried to
hammer the woodwork teacher, then you
hammered your father, then you
hammered yourself.

Norman Bates
Jekyll & Hyde
the Boston Strangler
Crippen & me.

First you tried to hammer the woodwork
teacher, then you hammered your father,
then you hammered yourself. Me a
hammer murderer. I wanted to explain
that it wasn't how it sounded, I wanted
to explain that it wasn't 1, 2, 3, hammer,
hammer, hammer without a pause for
breath, like he was saying it, like I was a
hammer murderer on the rampage. I
wanted to explain that it didn't happen
like that & then he said, 'Why did you
choose a hammer?'.

Oh lord I was scared then
I had to say over & over
I didn't choose a hammer
I never chose a hammer
it wasn't that I chose a hammer.

Norman Bates
Jekyll & Hyde
the Boston Strangler
Crippen & me
the hammer murderer

all in the Snake Pit
together.

(I was getting scared.)

I went to the psychiatrist & we all went
to family therapy. & my parents talked
& my sister talked & I said nothing, &
when the therapist asked me anything I
said I dunno. & I sat in the sessions like
I sat in the cupboard just waiting for the
time to go round.

& the weeks passed & the time went
round.

& my parents slowly stopped pressing me
& my parents slowly stopped getting at
    me
& my parents slowly stopped nagging &
    criticising me
& my parents slowly stopped punishing
    me
my parents slowly stopped.
& the school was tipped off & eased off
& my sister called me a loony when no
    one was around
& when the therapist asked if things were
    better
I said yes.
& they never asked about Benji
& then I stopped going to the
    psychiatrist.

& the weeks passed & the time went
round.

& when Benji & I felt like travelling
we went
& I didn't get into trouble anymore
& I never went into the cupboard again
& the eye for eye retributions stopped
& my schoolwork wasn't that important
    anymore
in fact my schoolwork wasn't important
    at all
nobody asked
& my parents expected nothing from me
& my sister called me a loony when no
    one was around
& the teachers chose to ignore me
& I chose to ignore the teachers
& Benji still sometimes stole but not
    often
& Benji still sometimes swore but only
    quietly
& we travelled a lot
& the time went round

& it still wasn't right.

You become aware of your lack of love
the lack of love you had as a child
you are aware of the lack of love as a
    child
& the anger grows because you are
    aware of the lack of love
& the wall gets stronger as awareness
    grows
the anger grows & the wall gets stronger
because you are aware of the lack of
    love
& the wall gets stronger & the anger
    grows
because you are aware of the adult
    power
you are aware of adult power & the lack
    of love
& the anger grows & the wall gets
    stronger
because frustration comes

When I was seventeen I thought the best
    thing to do was get out, get away,
    leave home,
I left.
I had always been a disappointment to
    my parents, a waste of effort, a
    failure, now I was a waste of space,
I left.
My parents bothered me, bugged me, let
    me do what I liked, put up with me
    silently, made me feel guilty,
I left.
It would be better, I would feel better, I
    could sort myself out, I could be free, I
    could be happy,
I thought.

It wasn't like that.

I lived in a bedsit
at first I had a job & then I didn't
I had no job, no money, no friends
I sat in my bedsit
my parents were quite good
sent me the odd tenner
through the post
never visited
I sat in my bedsit
sat in my bedsit
& slowly
went mad in my bedsit.

It started off fine, I felt good, relieved,
relaxed, I had no television but I wasn't
worried, I had the library & I had Benji.
She could come & go as she pleased
now, I no longer had to be careful of her
coming or going, I was no longer
guarded, or worried of how she or I
would appear to others, there were no
others. I sat & talked for hours with
Benji, talking about the past & the
future, how much better things were, a
million things we talked about & we
laughed a lot & went travelling,
travelling was cheap, we ate what we
wanted to eat when we wanted to eat it
& if we didn't feel like getting up in the
morning we didn't.
Occasionally I would think that I was too
old for imaginary friends, but mostly I
didn't think about it at all. It started off
fine, I felt good, relieved, relaxed. Then
Benji started getting restless, I could feel
her, things weren't really good, things
weren't really all right, we weren't
happy. We started arguing & she got on
my nerves as I got on her nerves & we
argued & we weren't happy, this wasn't
what we wanted. & we'd sit in silence for
hours, sit in silence, sit in a chair in
silence, sit in a chair in a bedsit in silence
for hours. We went out less & less until
we couldn't go out at all, didn't feel like
eating, didn't feel like reading, didn't feel
like travelling, didn't feel like talking.
Sat in a chair in a bedsit in silence for
hours. Benji was restless, she said the
bedsit was just a big cupboard, we were
just sitting in a big cupboard waiting for
the time to go round & it was
claustrophobic, we ought to get out, go
travelling, do something. We sat in a
chair in a bedsit in silence for hours &
couldn't move couldn't get out, couldn't
raise the energy. Benji was restless,
started shouting, arguing, the neighbours
complained & Benji got more restless,
started arguing with them, started singing
at the top of her voice in the middle of
the night. The neighbours complained
more & banged the walls & the door,
Benji swore & shouted & banged back.
& the neighbours complained & banged
& threatened & argued & Benji shouted
& sang & swore & screamed at all hours
of the day & night & then the police
came & I was sectioned.
Mental hospitals aren't that bad, they're
not bad at all, quite nice really, & not a
bit like the Snake Pit. Mind you I knew
that by then but even if it was like the

Snake Pit there wasn't much I could have done about it, not with Benji in control again. I was in a state & more or less resigned to the fact that I was a complete & utter lunatic, or more to the point completely possessed by an evil spirit called Benji. Maybe I didn't need a mental hospital but she did & since she was inside me I had to go along too. I was there for 6 weeks & they gave me some drugs to calm me down & I did calm down & I relaxed & Benji calmed down & faded a bit & I got a grip of myself & felt a lot better. It did me good, once I accepted that I was mental & went along with them. Everybody (well nearly everybody) was very nice & friendly & all the staff, the doctors & nurses & therapists & everybody said that if I had a problem I could always talk to them about it, which was very nice of them, very kind. There were a lot of people in that place that I could talk to if I had a problem. But I kept quiet & got calmer & got a grip of Benji & myself & felt better.

My parents & sister visited me once. That was embarrassing.

& then out
with a promise
to keep taking the medication
& go to outpatients
& do a little gardening job
& stay in the hostel.
It was decided
I should live in a hostel
be independent
but have help
close by
if required
somebody there
if I needed them
if I had a problem
if I had another breakdown.

The hostel warden was a bloke called Peter. Peter never once said if I had a problem I could talk to him about it. Peter never once assumed that I had a problem. Peter never mentioned problems either to me or to the other ex-patients. Peter would just chat. Anytime, all the time, whenever.
Peter helped.
Peter was a friend, all the people in the hostel were friends, it was a very friendly

atmosphere, I liked it. I felt like seven ex-mental-patients, a few staff members & Peter were my family. An odd family. A friendly family though.

& I lived with them for two years
& Benji was there
in the background at first
cus of the drugs
but as I slowly felt better
more secure
less in need
false security
I stopped taking them
thought I could manage without them
so Benji got stronger
more prominent
more out front
but friendly though
she was friendly for weeks
very popular
no trouble
false security.
Something went wrong
somebody did or said something wrong
or something happened, I'm not sure
but she started
angry, tantrum
flying off, sounding off
the usual
yelling & screaming & swearing
at my friends
my hostel family
at Peter
mostly at Peter
my friend
who stood there blinking
while Benji sounded off
while Benji threw a spanner in the works
while Benji ruined it all again
While Benji upset the balance
upset the family
upset my friends
upset me
cus I thought I'd be thrown out
cus I thought I'd be back in the bin
cus I thought she'd never die down
calm down, stay down
without drugs.

After she'd done her worst, burnt herself out, let me through, let me get control, let me speak, I apologised, tried to, spluttered & stuttered & tried to say sorry. Felt ashamed, felt terrible.

Peter said: we all get angry sometimes, its natural

no
yes
no you don't understand
it's all right, no damage done
but you don't understand
don't worry about it
but I do
you shouldn't, its OK, you were just
    letting off steam, that's all
no it isn't . . . it's Benji

& I told him.

I told him about Benji, I told him all
about Benji, how she was, who she was,
where she came from, everything. I told
him about how I decided to stop taking
my medication weeks ago even though I
knew I wasn't supposed to. I told him
about my family, my real family, my
parents always demanding perfection,
always expecting everything, how I
couldn't do it, how Benji ruined it for
me, How I loved my parents, how my
parents hated me. I told him about my
lady & how I'd loved her & how I missed
her even now & I never knew her name.
& I told him about everything,
everything I could think of just came
pouring out for hours & hours all day.
He listened. He listened & never once
said I was too old for imaginary friends
& he never said I was a loony & he
never said I shouldn't have stopped
taking the drugs, he listened. & over the
days afterwards when I wanted to say
some more he listened. & when
sometimes it was garbled & didn't make
sense he still listened but just asked me
to speak slower because he wanted to
know because he wanted to listen. & I
told him. He never once said I was too
old for imaginary friends, he never once
said I was loony, he never once said I
shouldn't have stopped taking the drugs,
he said once that maybe Benji was only
expressing what I felt. I didn't
understand at first but it made me think
about it.

It made me think a lot.

Frustration comes because you are no
    longer a child
you are no longer a child but you feel
    like a child
you feel like a child because you need

love like a child
you need love like a child because the
    child needed love
& the anger grows because the child
    needed love
& the anger grows because you need love
    like a child
& the anger grows because you are an
    adult
& the anger grows because frustration
    comes
& frustration comes because you are an
    adult
you are an adult but the child needs love
& the anger grows & the wall won't
    break
& the wall won't break because the
    anger won't stop
& the anger won't stop because you need
    love like a child
the child needs love to stop the anger
& you need love like a child to break the
    wall
you need to break the wall & stop the
    anger but you can't say
you can't say you need love like a child
you can't say because you are an adult
you can't say, you can't ask for love like
    a child
you can't ask because you are adult

I know now that I'm too old for
imaginary friends, I know that now.
I went back on the medication after the
little upset at the hostel, felt it was for
the best.
& then I got a flat, after the hostel, felt I
was ready, too old for imaginary friends,
hadn't needed Benji, hadn't even thought
about Benji, I had real friends now,
proper ones, not imaginary. & my doctor
agreed, said I was ready & they got me a
flat, a lovely flat & all my friends from
the hostel & Peter came & helped me
decorate & arrange the furniture, it was
good, I felt good, much too old for
imaginary friends.

But I was lonely in my flat
I missed my friends & Peter at the hostel
the noise & the commotion & the
    friendliness.
I'd visit them though
& they'd visit me, often
but after they'd gone
I couldn't bear it
the emptiness & silence

of just me
I'd never been on my own before
always had Benji
never been on my own.

Then I thought, this is silly, I'm just
being silly, I'm sure everybody feels like
this when they move into a new place,
bound to, I've just got to get used to it,
bound to feel strange, just got to keep
busy, keep myself occupied, not think
about it.

Didn't know what to do
then I thought 'why not go travelling?'
I've always enjoyed travelling
always made me feel better
cheered me up
But I couldn't
I tried
I did try
but I couldn't go
not without Benji
I missed her
couldn't go without her
Benji *was* travelling
couldn't bear it
I don't know, must have panicked
ran back
something
couldn't travel alone

I didn't know what to do, couldn't stay in
& couldn't go out. I was beginning to get
quite depressed. I was too old for
imaginary friends but I couldn't cope on
my own, I felt I just couldn't do it. & it
was just at that point, just at that point
when I thought I can't do it, can't cope,
have to go back to hospital or something,
it was just at that point that I had this
brilliant idea.

I thought 'why not get a dog?'
& I did.
I got a dog
& it's been brilliant
best thing I've ever done
I simply got a dog
& I can go travelling now
we go travelling, we go miles
me & my dog
& it's easy, no problem
I don't worry or panic
I don't even think about it
just off we go
& not dirty streets or buses any more
like with Benji

but parks & commons & places
I feel so healthy now too
I simply got a dog
should have done it years ago.

I'm so happy now, she makes me so
  happy.

& the flat. It doesn't seem empty or
silent or anything now, she doesn't say
anything but the flat feels so, I just love
it, I love going home to my flat now, &
it's all because of my dog.
& she's a real dog, she's not imaginary.
She is because I got her from Battersea
Dogs' Home & I couldn't imagine that
place it's so sad, so it's like I rescued
her, felt a real hero straight away.
I'm happy now, she's a great dog.
& it's funny cus ever since I've had her I
get this feeling that I'm close to my lady
again, not physically or anything I don't
mean that cus I don't know where she is
or anything, couldn't look her up even
don't know her name, but I mean in
spirit or something, like we connect
again, that she's near me, with me, I
don't know, maybe it's because we've
both got dogs, maybe we connect
through our dogs or something, I don't
know but it's just good to know she's
there, with me.
So I'm happy now.
& she's a great dog, not perfect though
thank god, nothing pedigree, just a
scruffy mongrel type, always into things,
a real scallywag. & we do everything
together, always together, just like Benji
was.
I do sometimes have this urge though, to
stop taking the medication, just for a
while, I don't mean for ever but just for
a little while, just so Benji could meet
her, I'd really like Benji to meet her, just
to see what she thought, to see if they'd
get on, cus I'm sure they would, cus
Benji's always liked dogs too, ever since
we met my lady & her dog, Benji, in fact
Benji was dead proud to be called after
Benji the dog, so I'm sure she'd like her.
Cus she's a great dog.
I'd also like Benji to come back just one
more time, just for the last time, because
I feel I want to apologise to her, I feel I
need to say sorry, cus I know now that it
wasn't Benji really, I know now that it
was me really, my anger, my emotion
that caused all that trouble, all that

wasted time, & I just feel I want to say
sorry for blaming her. Cus it wasn't her it
was me & I feel awful for blaming her, I
mean she was my best friend, she was,
she was my best friend & I blamed her
all those years, so I would just like to say
sorry.
& I'd like to say goodbye.
But I can't, I can't even think about it, I
mustn't think about it, cus I'm too old
for imaginary friends, I've got to keep
taking the medication cus it is for the
best, so I shouldn't think about Benji or
the past or anything, I should just think
about my dog, well I do think about my
dog in fact, I do, I concentrate on my
dog & try to make her happy, cus she
makes me happy, she does, she's a great
dog, a real scallywag, always into
everything, messing up the flat with her
dog hairs & everything, I can't keep the
place clean I can't, everytime I try to
clean the floor or anything she's there
with her paw prints all over it. She's a
real monster & a horror & a terror she
is.
I call her Lady.
It's just a name.

Adult Child/Dead Child

I would find it difficult to write plays on a specific theme. That is, I would be hard pushed if somebody said write about 'such and such' a thing. So I find it incredibly satisfying and surprising when something comes out that is *about* something. And even happier when it seems to be about lots of things.

What I liked specifically about performing this play was the number of people who came up to me after the show and told me what it meant for them. Some, obviously, thought it was simply about a schizophrenic character, others didn't see the mental illness at all, just loneliness and an inability to make oneself understood. Others thought it said a lot about childhood and how everybody is affected by other people's ideals, though not necessarily to the same degree as the character in this play! Some saw it as the beginnings and buildup of a violent person. One woman even thought it was fascinating to see how troubled a person can become through hating their parents (which made *me* think a bit). Personally I'm not too sure what the play's about except what social animals humans are, and the devices we create to meet our social needs, and how even our own creations can let us down and confuse us.

It was also interesting while performing the piece to find how different I felt each night, depending on what sort of audience was watching and how different parts of the play struck me more emphatically than during other performances. I sometimes think that an audience underestimates the role it plays in dictating how an evening is going to turn out – I don't believe there's such a thing as passive viewing in the theatre! For instance, playing to an audience that was approximately 80 per cent women, I found myself much more open and willing to express the vulnerability of the character, whereas where there were more men than women in the audience my performances lent more to the comic side than the emotional. (This is, of course, very much a generalisation; the difference in performance was more subtle than that.) Funnily enough, the strangest performance was a night when the audience was mainly professionals from the psychiatric field; the feeling that pervaded that night was incredibly clinical, slightly austere, not the least bit helpful or giving and made me feel very much like a specimen to be analysed. Not that I'm saying anything against members of the psychiatric profession personally, but collectively – they're terrifying!

A lot of people asked me why the character was androgenous (or more to the point, a lot of 'feminist' women asked why I didn't make the character blatantly female), which seems odd to me since I didn't know that loneliness, lovelessness, misunderstanding and mishandling only applied to women. It can and does happen to anybody, regardless of gender, although I will admit that a woman is expected to conform more to other people's ideals and is pressured to please people, particularly those around her, in spite of her natural character and spirit. But I think that any situation in which people of any gender are forced to repress their true feelings and are unable or not allowed to express their emotions can lead to some kind of mental overload. This seems to say more about our society and particularly our society's view of women that it does about mental illness. In that sense this is a feminist play that equally concerns men, which is how I think feminism should be.

Another thing I found whilst performing the piece was the number of people who asked whether it was autobiographical (I talked to an awful lot of people during this play). To that I say 'what difference does it make?'

Claire Dowie started off as a poet
became a comedian
ran out of punchlines
so started writing plays.

Her first play was *Cat and Mouse* (1987), about the lack of communication between father and son in coming to terms with sexual abuse.

STAMPING, SHOUTING AND SINGING HOME

Lisa Evans

Characters

PERFORMER 1: Lizzie
PERFORMER 2: Marguerite, Sojourner,
PERFORMER 3: Mama, Louella
PERFORMER 4: Uncle Chrystal, Joanne, Teacher, Preacher, Heckler, Cop

Setting
On stage there are one costume trunk and one tin trunk.

Stamping, Shouting and Singing Home was commissioned and first performed by Watford Palace Theatre-in-Education Company on 14 May 1986 at Kings Langley School, Kings Langley, Herts, with the following cast:

LIZZIE	Clare Perkins
MARGUERITE }	Vinny Dhillon
SOJOURNER TRUTH }	
MAMA }	Janice McKenzie
LOUELLA }	
UNCLE CHRYSTAL }	Fiona Branson
JOANNE }	

Directed by Gwenda Hughes
Designed by Nettie Scriven
Musical Director Andrew Dodge
Stage Manager Gavin Stride
Administration by Dot Butcher

ACT ONE

Scene One

Song: 'Let My People Go'.

LIZZIE: The time, it is summer. The place, oh someplace in the deep South. And the story? Been told before, be told again. And I, knee-high to a bug, walk, feet bare, step step down the dusty track past the fields humming with Sunday quiet. And the singing, so's their hearts would break, coming from the black folks' church, as I slip away past the hot sun and into the wood. And ain't I grown enough to walk alone? Lord you could be buried in the green in this swampy place. Summer's been growing along a month or so now. Out among the cotton it's as hot as Africa where the stories come, so Mama tells it. The time, the beginning, the place, my home, and me – Lizzie Walker – picking flowers like there's no tomorrow. Look at the bunch I got me already. Can't hear the singing no more, close in the wood. Hum to myself instead, picking the silver ferns and flowers blue as white folks' eyes. Hear my mama saying . . .

MAMA: You mind out for snakes now, you hear?

LIZZIE: Stop by this big ole tree, bark all mossy green and damp. Been here since before the Indians even, I reckon. If there was such a time. Looking up I sees the patchwork pieces of sky. Seems God left a thread dangling. Hanging frayed from a branch. It was then his foot touched my cheek. Except it wasn't like no foot I ever seen. Just bones charred black. The bones of what was once his hands outstretched like he's still begging for life. Big hands. A working man. Could have been a brother. Necklace of barbed wire still clinging round his jaw as he swings gentle, what was once a man, over what was once a fire. He should be buried proper. Seem like his story over and done with sure enough. Sure enough summer over too.

Song: 'Let My People Go'.

Scene Two

As LIZZIE speaks she unpacks key props/items of clothing from the trunk and hands them to the other performers.

LIZZIE: And here I am now, unpacking the past. Trunk full of history, old clothes my family wore I can't bear to throw away. The attic's full of them. And a feather duster my Great Uncle Chrystal used for the training of cats. Marguerite's scarf, Mama's pinafore and this jacket. Well, it belonged to my big brother Charles. Only he's dead now. He was killed fighting across the world. But you'll get to hear about him all the same. In my family there's dead folk hopping in and outa the conversation all the time. Mama would sit in her rocker, wrapped in her shawl, sewing the quilt and telling tales of my great-granma and her mama, Sojourner Truth, and sisters stretching back in time, way back, across the seas to Africa where we began. So many sisters, so many stories. And my sister, whose middle name was Trouble. But we generally called her Marguerite. She was bigger than me and badder than me and she answered back all the time and got away with it. Mama'd say . . .

MAMA: You just like your great-great-granma, Sojourner Truth.

LIZZIE: Wasn't nobody got the better of Sojourner, spite the fact she born a slave who never learned to read nor write.

And then there was me, Lizzie Walker, just trying to reach a mark a bit higher up the barn door each summer, just trying to get along on my own story without any trouble. Let me tell you one thing, sure enough, that ain't easy coming youngest in a long line of wilful women. Seems once folk gotten into the way of being active, it's awful hard keeping them down.

Scene Three

MAMA: Lizzie, Marguerite, you ready for school?

LIZZIE:
MARGUERITE: } Yes Mama.

MAMA: Schooling teaches you how to think. You lucky we allowed a school for coloured folk. Off you go now.

*Song: 'Battle Hymn of the Republic',
as first* MARGUERITE *and then*
LIZZIE *move to school.*

TEACHER: You all pay attention now.
Lizzie Walker, you're late again.
Dreaming I suppose.

LIZZIE: No ma'am,

TEACHER: Today is history. H-I-S-T-
O-R-Y.

MARGUERITE: Lizzie.

TEACHER: John Brown. B-R-O-W-N.

LIZZIE: What?

MARGUERITE: There's a cockroach
heading up your skirt.

LIZZIE: Where!

TEACHER: Lizzie Walker, what are
you doing?

LIZZIE: Just looking ma'am.

TEACHER: Well don't. What do you
know about John Brown?

MARGUERITE: *(Singing)*: His body lies
a mouldering in the grave but his soul
goes marching on. Ma'am.

TEACHER: I won't have no singing of
that kind here. John Brown was a
fanatic. A traitor. Who knows what
that means?

MARGUERITE: He's bad, ma'am?

TEACHER: Yes, Marguerite. He was a
crazy man. He talked poor coloured
men who didn't know no better into a
riot. They were shot by the forces of
law and order.

LIZZIE: I don't see no roach.

TEACHER: Lizzie Walker!

LIZZIE: Yes, ma'am.

TEACHER: What is law and order?

LIZZIE: Doing as you're told, ma'am?

TEACHER: Mm. By who?

LIZZIE: White folks?

TEACHER: By the sheriff, the state
police and the government.

MARGUERITE (*to* Lizzie): That's white
folks.

LIZZIE: Oh.

MARGUERITE: Your roach gone

marching up your back, Lizzie.

LIZZIE: Where?

MARGUERITE: I seen his whiskers
waving.

LIZZIE: Marguerite, if you telling me
stories, you going to go to hell.

MARGUERITE: It's the truth.

TEACHER: He was hanged on
December 2nd 1859 by the neck until
he was dead.

LIZZIE: I can't see it.

MARGUERITE: Waving his legs now.
About to bite your ear, poison your
blood.

LIZZIE *leaps up screeching and
flapping.*

TEACHER: Lizzie Walker you come
here to learn, not fool around!

LIZZIE: She said I had a cockroach up
my back, ma'am. I couldn't sit still
knowing he marching up and down my
spine.

TEACHER: I'll give you marching, right
out of this class! Let me see.

MARGUERITE: It was a roach.

TEACHER: Marguerite, you telling lies?

MARGUERITE: No ma'am, there was
a roach, swear to God.

TEACHER: Sit down, Lizzie, and you
pay attention, Marguerite. I am
attempting to teach you history. That's
spelled H-I-S – Marguerite?

MARGUERITE: His.

TEACHER: Then story. His story.
What's that?

MARGUERITE: It's the truth, ma'am.
Written in books, like the Bible and
all.

TEACHER: And the people who wrote
these books were people who knew.
Clever people. People in command of
the facts. Class dismissed.

LIZZIE: } Thank you Miss
MARGUERITE: } Wescott.

LIZZIE: Please ma'am.

TEACHER: What is it?

LIZZIE: Did black folks ever write these
books, history?

TEACHER: How could they, most of them couldn't read nor write?

LIZZIE: Oh.

MARGUERITE: Come on.

MARGUERITE *and* LIZZIE *move away.* TEACHER *leaves.*

LIZZIE: Was there really a roach?

MARGUERITE: Yes.

LIZZIE: You be going to get struck by a thunderbolt if you lie.

MARGUERITE: I seen him, scuttling across the floor.

LIZZIE: And?

MARGUERITE: I didn't tell her no lie. I just said there was a roach. That's the truth.

LIZZIE: What about when it done run up my back?

MARGUERITE: I didn't tell the teacher that.

LIZZIE: You told me!

MARGUERITE: I sort of imagined what the roach might do if it had a mind.

LIZZIE: It's just as well you can't write good yet, Marguerite, cos you put that down in letters and sure as hell you going to get hit by that thunderbolt. Blow you further up the road than a cottonball in the wind.

Song: 'John Brown's Body'.

In between the verses as the tin bath is brought out LIZZIE *speaks.*

In the next part of my story I ain't got no clothes and this is full of water.

LIZZIE *climbs fully dressed into the empty bath.*

Scene Four

MARGUERITE *is drying her hair.* MAMA *is washing* LIZZIE *in the tin tub. It is not* LIZZIE'S *favourite night of the week.*

MAMA: And like Sojourner's mama say to her I say to you, see the stars, those are the same stars and that is the same moon that look down upon your brothers and sisters, and which they see as they look up at them though they ever so far away from us and each other. For her brothers and sisters were sold away from home to other slave owners before they even as big as you. And when she nine years old Sojourner she sold away from home too, to a man who bought her along with a flock of sheep. A man who gave her no shoes so her feet froze like the river in winter. While Sojourner sleeping on straw and crying for cold her mama done die and, big deal, Sojourner allowed to go visit her pa for the funeral. Just one day though and back to work and being beaten day and night with rods tied together. One day she gets sold, for $70 cos she a good worker, better than a man her master say. She washing all the white family's clothes in the night-time and hoeing and raking in the fields all day. This new master look at Sojourner, big and strong, and he thinks 'this slave be right for breeding'. So he picks one of his men slaves and he says, 'I decided, you two married now'. And in time Sojourner, she have five children, five new brown workers. But things is changing. The law says on July 4th Sojourner going to be free. She wait so eager for this day but when it come, the master say 'You was sick a while back. You gotta make up that time afore I set you free.' Suddenly, been told before, be told again, Sojourner see the light. He ain't never going to free her. So she pick up the smallest baby with one arm and a bundle of belongings with the other and she run away. Sojourner learned, ain't no good sitting and waiting on some master to give you freedom. You got to take it. And then, like Harriet, you got to give it away to other brothers and sisters, time and time again.

LIZZIE *is now out of the bath and being dried.*

LIZZIE: Who were Harriet and Sojourner, Mama, are they history?

MAMA: Yes.

LIZZIE: Then why ain't they in the books?

MAMA: Lots of ordinary folks got left out, honey. They still there – like Sojourner speaking her truth and Harriet Tubman setting folks free.

LIZZIE: And I looked at the history books and found she was right. Nobody wrote nothing about me and my kind. Seemed like someone decided we didn't exist. Goes to show how wrong some people can be.

Scene Five

On the verandah. Two white women sipping cold drinks served to them by MARGUERITE.

LOUELLA: I don't know what's the matter in this town today, really I don't.

JOANNE: Mary, don't forget the shirts must be starched again. My husband is very particular.

MARGUERITE: Yes, ma'am.

MARGUERITE *exits.*

LOUELLA: They're getting so uppity. Grinning from ear to ear. Our menfolks won't stand for it. There'll be trouble tonight, mark my words, Joanne. Mark them.

JOANNE: It's all on account of that fight I daresay. Like children.

LOUELLA: My, this heat's enough to tire a body out.

They sip their drinks.

JOANNE: Mary! There's not enough sugar in this. Mary!

MARGUERITE *enters wiping her hands.*

MARGUERITE: Yes, ma'am?

JOANNE: Don't come to the table wiping your hands, Mary. Sugar.

MARGUERITE: You said you wanted less, for the weight, ma'am.

JOANNE: Don't cheek me, girl.

MARGUERITE: No, ma'am.

MARGUERITE *exits.*

JOANNE: Mary! Cussedness! Mary! When I took her on, out of the goodness of my heart, she tells me her name's Marguerite, or some such foolishness.

LOUELLA: Marguerite. My, they do have such fancy names.

JOANNE: Too fancy. And too long. I can't be shouting Marguerite all day long. So I call her Mary. It's simpler.

LOUELLA: What fight were you talking about, Joanne dear? In the street here in town? I didn't hear nothing.

MARGUERITE *enters.*

JOANNE: Some boy won some boxing fight, that's all. Everyone reckoned the title-holder would win, then back comes this Louis, hits him for the count.

LOUELLA: Was he a black?

JOANNE: Yes. Mary, why didn't you answer me?

MARGUERITE: Ma'am?

JOANNE: I have better ways to spend my time than call after you.

LOUELLA: What was that black boy's name?

MARGUERITE: Joe Louis, ma'am! The sugar.

MARGUERITE *sweeps the yard.*

JOANNE: If she wasn't such a hard worker I'd have fired her weeks ago.

JOANNE *ladles sugar into her drink.*

MARGUERITE: Into the ring. Round One.

JOANNE: Sugar, Louella?

LOUELLA: No thank you, dear. I can't abide fighting.

JOANNE *takes a mouthful of the drink and chokes.*

There there, dear.

JOANNE (*gasping*): Salt. She brought salt!

LOUELLA: Oh dear. Mary! Mary, bring some water for your mistress, you wicked girl.

MARGUERITE: Round Two! He's off the ropes, ladies and gentlemen. He's moving up towards the centre of the ring.

LOUELLA: Fetch water, girl!

MARGUERITE: And now it looks like Louis getting mad. There's a left cross, and a right to the head.

LOUELLA: She's gone stone crazy, Joanne.

MARGUERITE: Eight, nine, ten . . . and it's Joe Louis the winner and Heavyweight Champion of the World!

JOANNE: Stop it at once, Mary!

MARGUERITE: Ma'am.

JOANNE: You're going to get such a whipping for this, Mary.

LOUELLA: A whipping, do you hear?

JOANNE: Fetch the switch, Mary. And one word from you and you'll be leaving, not just here but town. Isn't nobody going to give you work if I say not.

MARGUERITE: Yes, ma'am.

LOUELLA: It shouldn't be allowed. It gives them ideas. Champion of the World indeed.

JOANNE: I'm going to tame you good and proper.

MARGUERITE: No, ma'am. You going to tame Mary. My name's Marguerite.

Song: 'No More Moaning'.

Scene Six

At home. MARGUERITE enters. LIZZIE watches the following scene, bringing MAMA the bowl and cloth to bathe MARGUERITE's back.

MAMA: You gave her salt instead of sugar?

MARGUERITE: Yes.

MAMA: A mistake?

MARGUERITE: Mn hm.

MAMA: C'mon over here, Trouble.

Matter-of-factly MAMA bathes MARGUERITE's back, her anger and what-to-do-about-it-all coming out in her positive story about Harriet.

MARGUERITE: Ow.

MAMA: Hold still. Now the way the story goes, the overseer calls to Harriet, 'Stop that man! Runaway slave! I'm going to whip him till he know his place!' And Harriet see this slave, head down and running. He goes past her and through the door. A brother breaking free. Now Harriet she don't think, she just act. And she move in front of that door, blocking the overseer's path. Stands like a rock. Mad as hell, the overseer picks up a two-pound weight and hurls it. It catch Harriet square on her forehead knocking her unconscious near to death. From harvest past Christmas she lay in the slave cabin, not moving, like a stone. And come spring she wake up and there begins the story of another sister – Harriet Tubman – who ran away to Canada and then came back, again and again. Dressed as a man for a price higher than gold was on her head – and lead her people along the river-banks, cross miles of slave-owning land, with dogs baying after them, in danger and darkness. And all the while keeping their spirits going with songs of freedom. And each time she come back she'd whistle outside the cabins, low and quiet

LIZZIE whistles two lines of 'Go Down Moses'.
as a sign she'd come to lead more brothers and sisters north out of slavery. And for this they called her Moses. A small black woman with no learning and a deep hole in her forehead marking the price she pay to say no for the first time.

MARGUERITE: It don't hurt so much now, Mama.

MAMA: Salt instead of sugar huh?

Song: 'Oh Freedom'.

Scene Seven

MAMA *is cutting up old pieces of material for her quilt. LIZZIE is reading the Bible.*

LIZZIE: 'And the Lord said unto the woman, what is this that thou hast done? I will greatly multiply thy sorrow . . .' What's that one, Mama?

MAMA: That? I think it's your granma's wedding dress.

LIZZIE: But it's all patterns.

MAMA: She love your granpa just the same. Get along with your reading Lizzie.

LIZZIE: 'thy conception, in sorrow thou shalt bring forth children; and thy desire shall be to thy husband and he shall rule over thee.' What's rule, Mama?

MAMA: It's when one set of folks tells another set of folks what to do.

LIZZIE: Was Adam white?

MAMA: No child, he was just a man.

LIZZIE: Oh. Mama, why didn't God like Eve?

MAMA: She eaten of the tree of knowledge, she know too much. Go find your sister now.

LIZZIE: I been running around all day.

MAMA: Then walk. You got the name for it. Walker.

LIZZIE: I'm tired.

MAMA: And you ain't even started yet. Sojourner walked everywhere.

LIZZIE: Well I bet she got tired too sometimes.

MAMA: I reckon she did. Tired of hearing the same old excuses, same as I do!

LIZZIE: Tell me a story, Mama. About Sojourner.

MAMA: Well . . . oh, you are one daughter of Eve and no mistake – real clever. But so am I. So go get Marguerite and then I'll tell you about how Sojourner stood up for old Eve. Now get along!

MAMA *leaves.*

Scene Eight

LIZZIE: Marguerite! Marguerite!

Getting no response, LIZZIE *starts to play hopscotch with an imaginary person. She goes first.*

Your turn.
And no cheating. Ah ah. My turn now and I going to win.

MARGUERITE *enters reading a newspaper in which she is engrossed.*

Mama wants you. She sent me out to get you.

MARGUERITE: I can see you been looking real hard.

LIZZIE: I'm winning.

She continues her game.

MARGUERITE: Who you playing with?

LIZZIE: Never you mind.

MARGUERITE: There's nobody there.

LIZZIE: Yes there is.

MARGUERITE: Who then?

LIZZIE: God.

MARGUERITE: You playing hopscotch against God!

LIZZIE: Yes. And I'm winning. Where you been?

MARGUERITE: Reading.

LIZZIE: Me too. All about how God give Eve a real hard time cos she went talking to a snake.

MARGUERITE *goes back to reading her paper.*

MARGUERITE: Uh huh.

LIZZIE: I wouldn't talk to no snake. Eve must have been real lonely talking to a dumb creature. I reckon Adam wasn't much good at passing the time of day. Probably too busy combing his hair, like Charles.

MARGUERITE: What?

LIZZIE: Well, like Charles used to, fore he went to the war. Can't you just picture it?

(*As Eve:*) Hi Adam, nice day. Looks like it might rain. Big storm clouds approaching over Eden.

(*As Adam combing his hair:*) Uh huh.

(*As Eve:*) Yea, I reckon that cloud going to break soon. Going to be one wet weekend in Eden all right. What d'ya say we go someplace else for the day?

(*As Adam:*) Uh huh.

(*As Eve:*) Course if you don't reckon much to that, we could just lie around here watching the apples fall off the tree.

(*As Adam:*) Uh huh.

(*As Eve:*) Or I guess I could just go talk to a snake.

(*As Adam:*) OK. You do that.

You listening, Marguerite?

MARGUERITE: Uh huh.

LIZZIE: So anyways Eve has this real good conversation with this snake about how apples is good for your teeth and all and I spect she moans on a bit about how Adam spend all his time combing his hair and not paying her no attention. . .

MARGUERITE: There's going to be a march here in town.

LIZZIE: That right? Well, it's just coming on to evening and Eve sees she was right about the weather, sure enough. So she calls out to Adam, 'Hey, Adam, it's going to rain like hell and you going to catch your death out there with no clothes on, you hear!' And WHAM! Down come God on a thunderbolt and kicks them out of their house in Eden and all cos Adam wasn't no good at making conversation. Whatcha think?

MARGUERITE: I think I ought to go.

LIZZIE: Go where?

MARGUERITE: On the march.

LIZZIE: You kidding! Folks gets in trouble for that. We got to get home.

MARGUERITE: No news about his regiment in the paper.

LIZZIE (*going back to playing hopscotch*): Who?

MARGUERITE: Charles of course. Your brother, remember?

LIZZIE: Oh yea, that Charles. I spect he going to come home a hero anyways.

MARGUERITE: Just so long as he come home.

LIZZIE: What for? So's he can pull your hair again and twist your arm fit to break? I don't care if he never come back.

MARGUERITE *shakes* LIZZIE.

MARGUERITE: Don't you ever dare say that again Lizzie Walker, you hear me!

LIZZIE: Let me go!

MARGUERITE: He's your brother.

LIZZIE: So? You my sister and you shaking me to bits. What's so fine about brothers and sisters?

MARGUERITE: Ask Mama.

LIZZIE: I shall so too.

MARGUERITE *leaves*.

Like I said, just being dead don't keep you out of family conversation. Fact is you probably gets more air time that way.

Like Sojourner and her chosen name of Truth.

LIZZIE *gets the patchwork quilt and helps* MAMA *unfold it*.

Scene Nine

LIZZIE *listens as* MAMA *tells the story*.

MAMA: And when Sojourner enter the meeting hall they all turns and looks. Six feet tall of woman and black woman at that, in her Quaker bonnet and long skirts.

SOJOURNER *enters*.

She look at the speakers sitting up on the platform and at the crowd assembled and something ain't right. They supposed to be talking about women's rights and all the folks who are talking and hollering is men, and church men at that. And they say . . .

WHITE HECKLER: If God wanted the equality of women he'd have made them strong as men!

Jesus was a man!

It was Eve caused Adam to be thrown out of Eden!

MAMA: Now Sojourner, she keep quiet for one whole day of this nonsense. Come day two, she rise slowly to her feet and move to the centre of the platform. They try to stop her with their shouting. But Sojourner got something to say. She silence them with one long look.

SOJOURNER: Well children, where there is so much racket there must be something out of kilter. Between the negroes in the South and the white men in the North all talking about rights, you white men will be in a fix pretty soon. But what's all this talking about?

MAMA: At which they starts shouting again.

WHITE HECKLER: If women need seats in carriages and strong arms to help them, they don't need rights!

MAMA: Sojourner's eyes flash like thunderbolts.

SOJOURNER: That man over there says that women need to be helped into carriages and lifted over ditches, and to have the best place everywhere. Nobody ever helps me into carriages, or over mud puddles, or gives me any best place, and ain't I a woman? Look at me! Look at my arm! I have ploughed and planted and gathered into barns, and no man could head me – and ain't I a woman? I could work as much and eat as much as a man (when I could get it) and bear the lash as well – and ain't I a woman? I have borne five children and seen them most all sold off into slavery, and when I cried out with a mother's grief, none but Jesus heard – and ain't I a woman?

MAMA: And ain't I a woman.

WHITE HECKLER: Jesus was a man!

SOJOURNER: Jesus was born from God and a woman. Man had nothin to do with it.

MAMA: She got him there.

WHITE HECKLER: What about Eve and the serpent? Women is trouble!

MAMA: You bet she got an answer for that too.

SOJOURNER: If the first woman God ever made was strong enough to turn the world upside down, all alone, all these women here together ought to be able to turn it back and get it right side up again, and now they're asking to do it . . .

MAMA: The men better let them!

LIZZIE: Well, if Mama and Sojourner thought old Eve was one fine woman, far as I concerned, she was. You know, seems to me Joe Louis, champion fighter and Sojourner Truth got a lot in common. And on account of the stories, which kept on coming, the fighting didn't stop there. Like the evening sister Marguerite didn't come home. It was a Saturday, always a bad night as Mama did the accounts.

Scene Ten

MAMA *is doing the accounts*, LIZZIE *has a bag of sweets and is reading the Bible.*

MAMA: Milk, meal, cornstarch makes $3.20. We going to have to cut down.

LIZZIE: I knew where Marguerite been going, but I wasn't telling. Not me.

MAMA: Where is that girl, it's past nightfall?

LIZZIE: Who, Mama?

MAMA: Don't you act womanish with me, Lizzie Walker.

LIZZIE: Me, Mama?

I was really living dangerous. I pretended to be reading but I could feel Mama's eyes boring holes in the top of my head. It gone real quiet.

MAMA: Lizzie?

LIZZIE: Yes, Mama?

MAMA: Tell me the part of the Bible you learned yesterday.

LIZZIE: Her voice like oil. Better watch out.

Which part Mama?

MAMA: About how the first wrote.

LIZZIE: 'The first wrote, wine is the strongest
The second wrote, the King is strongest
The third wrote, women are strongest.'

I liked that. I was strong. I wasn't telling no tales.

MAMA: Wasn't there another line?

LIZZIE: Was there?

MAMA: I think so, don't you?

LIZZIE: She got me.
'But above all things Truth beareth away the victory.'

MAMA: So where is Marguerite?

LIZZIE: Now there's times when you just got to stand your ground.

MAMA: Lizzie.

LIZZIE: I don't know.

MAMA: Elizabeth.

LIZZIE: And times you just got to admit defeat. Down the white folks' end of town.

MAMA: And you sat here all evening knowing this and never saying a word?!

LIZZIE: I promised.

MAMA: Hold your tongue! Doesn't she know how dangerous that is? She been sleepwalking all her life? Saturday night and the white men out in their cars drinking and looking for trouble. Well, doesn't she know?

LIZZIE: Marguerite said . . .

MAMA: Don't answer me back!

LIZZIE (*to the audience*): How come it's Marguerite's done wrong and I'm the one getting hollered at?

MAMA: Don't she know she crying out for trouble? That girl got less sense than a nodding dog. And as for you!

LIZZIE: It was about this time I got real interested in my reading.

Her head is virtually inside her Bible.

MAMA: And she went out wearing nothing but a thin dress. If she come home, please Lord, soaked through with pneumonia, she needn't think I'm going to sit up day and night nursing her. Oh no.

MAMA *puts on her hat.*

LIZZIE: I could tell we in for a bumpy night. Mama putting on her going-into-battle-hat.

MAMA: I prayed to the Lord to send me children and what do I get? Chicken brains, that's what! Charles playing soldiers and shooting at yellow people halfway cross the world, Marguerite gallivanting around all night where she didn't ought to be, getting herself beat up and run over, taking to drink and being abused . . .

LIZZIE: Mama, you don't know that for sure.

MAMA: Don't tell me what I know! She lying murdered in some ditch this very minute for certain. And then she going to walk home alone on that road in the pitch dark. When she come in, please Lord, I'm going to give her such a hiding she won't know Thursday from Christmas!

LIZZIE: Shall I read to you, Mama?

MAMA: Yes.

MAMA *Doesn't listen.*

LIZZIE: 'And in the time of their visitation they shall shine, and run to and fro like sparks among the stubble. And so . . .'

MARGUERITE *enters.*

Marguerite!

MAMA: Baby, where have you been?

LIZZIE: And Marguerite she just stands there in the doorway, rain or something running down her cheeks, clothes clinging to her bones like a cat someone tried to drown. And she don't say nothing.

MAMA *puts the quilt round* MARGUERITE.

MAMA: Are you hurt?

MARGUERITE *shakes her head.*

Did anyone abuse you child?

MARGUERITE *shakes her head.*

Well where in the name of heaven you been!?

LIZZIE: Mama about to start blowing like the wind whistling outside when something in Marguerite's look stops her. Seems like it's my sister's turn to tell her story.

MARGUERITE: I went to the coffee shop.

MAMA: But that's a white folks' place.

MARGUERITE: Law says it isn't.

MAMA: Law! Why, honey?

MARGUERITE: I wanted to drink coffee.

LIZZIE: What happened?

MAMA: Ssh. Let her tell it like it was.

MARGUERITE: I didn't plan on staying out late, Mama. It was light when I went in. It was real crowded but only a few folks sitting outside at them pretty tables on the sidewalk. So I went and sat there too. Folks were staring like I come from Mars or someplace. You think my skin green not brown. But I didn't take notice. I sat at the table and waited for the waitress. Pretty soon she come out and took an order from the table next to mine. Then she goes back inside. Through the glass I could see white folks nudging and laughing at me, and the waitress talking to the manager. She come out with the order for the next table. This time I say, 'Excuse me miss'. But she act like I wasn't there. No voice. No sound. But I heard my voice. And I heard it again when next she pass and I say, very polite, 'I'd like a cup of coffee, please'. I ask three more times but she carries on acting like I'm invisible. Then it come on to rain. But I sat on. I sat on while it got dark and they turned up the lights inside. And folks came and went and had coffee and cake and talked and laughed together. And I sat on. Pretending I didn't care. They weren't going to drive me away. Flood could have come and I'd have stayed, sitting in the dark, rain on the window panes, running down my back till I didn't rightly know if I was turned to stone. Some cars hooted as they drove off, laughing and yelling foul words. But I sat on. I had a right to be sitting there. I had a right to be served coffee just like they did. So I sat on. Then they closed up, put out the lights. I got up and come home.

LIZZIE *looks in her bag of sweets. There is one left. She gives it to* MARGUERITE.

Song: 'Hush You Bye'.

ACT TWO

Scene One

Song: 'Take This Hammer'.

LIZZIE: My great-great-granma was a slave and all her family too and the way they taught me in school they all had a pretty good time of it. A place to live, all their food and plenty of smiling black folks picking cotton and singing along under the southern sun.

First verse of 'She Know Moon-rise', sung by all:

Our Ritt'll walk in the starlight
She'll walk in the starlight
To lay her body down.

LIZZIE: And so the seasons went past with no worries and no responsibilities. Seedtime, cotton blossom time, harvest and Christmas. All in the service of King Cotton.

Second verse of 'She Know Moon-rise':

Our Ritt'll walk in the graveyard
She'll walk through the graveyard
To lay her body down.

LIZZIE: And yet and still they taught me the slaves kept on smiling, praising the Lord, picking the fleecy white cotton and keeping the big houses with their wide verandahs so clean they ready for white-glove inspection.

Third verse of 'She Know Moon-rise':

Our Ritt'll lie in the graveyard
Stretch out her arms in the graveyard
To lay her body down.

LIZZIE: Truth beareth away the victory. If you can't dance it and you can't sing it, leastways it ought to be told right. When my grandma got active those white men come and dug up her ma's grave. Dumped her dust in the front yard. Found a splinter of finger bone among the marigolds. I'll tell it and tell it right. You see, I owe it to those who walked before and those on the road to come.

Chorus of 'She Know Moon-rise':

She know moon-rise
She know star-rise
But she done lay her body down.

LIZZIE: Truth was, things beginning to hot up. Marguerite's getting active, causing trouble. Mind, she'd been that way since I could remember. Since she started telling me I had cockroaches crawling down my back. Now though it was other folks she got scratching. Like the day Miz Joanne come home from the hospital and got bit by the snake.

Scene Two

LOUELLA *and* JOANNE *are lolling on the verandah, fanning themselves.*

LOUELLA: How many pints you say you lost Joanne?

JOANNE: Altogether I had to be given thirteen pints of blood.

LOUELLA: All at the same time?

JOANNE: Don't be foolish, Louella. Thirteen wouldn't fit all at once.

LOUELLA: I was wondering. You'd have looked like a bullfrog.

JOANNE: I have been a very sick woman Louella, kindly don't upset me with your jokes.

MARGUERITE *enters carrying a bunch of herbs and speaks to* LOUELLA.

MARGUERITE: Morning, ma'am.

JOANNE: Where have you been Mary, I've been calling and calling.

MARGUERITE: How you doing, ma'am?

LOUELLA: Thank you, just fine.

JOANNE: Mary, I asked you a question!

MARGUERITE: I'll just take these herbs on down to the kitchen.

JOANNE: Mary!

MARGUERITE *exits.*

LOUELLA: Don't you go upsetting yourself now, Joanne. You're a sick woman. Eleven pints remember.

JOANNE: Thirteen. I had thirteen. And all of it white.

LOUELLA: No Joanne, dear. Blood's red.

JOANNE: I said to them as they were putting the needle in my arm. No black blood. I die first. Then I saw the needle and fainted clean away. I've always

been of a delicate nature you know. MARY!

LOUELLA: I'm wondering if perhaps the sun's too strong out here on the porch, Joanne dear.

JOANNE: I need a drop of Southern Comfort for my strength. MARY!

LOUELLA: Now quieten down, dear. I'll fetch her. You rest up.

JOANNE: Oh very well.

LOUELLA: (*Quietly*): Marguerite?

MARGUERITE *appears instantly.*

MARGUERITE: Yes, ma'am?

LOUELLA: Miss Joanne would like a glass of spirits.

MARGUERITE: She ain't allowed no strong liquor, doctor said.

MARGUERITE *gives* JOANNE *a drink.*

You have a sip of that, ma'am. Do you a power of good.

JOANNE: What is it?

MARGUERITE: To keep your spirits up.

JOANNE (*brightens*) Spirit?

LOUELLA (*fanning herself*): We all need our spirits up in these hard times. I declare we do.

JOANNE *takes a mouthful and spits it out.*

JOANNE: Take it away!

MARGUERITE: I know it tastes a little bitter, but it's real good for you, ma'am.

JOANNE: She's trying to poison me!

LOUELLA: Oh I shouldn't think so, Joanne, she'd be out of a job if she did.

JOANNE: Take that away. I ain't drinking no poisonous witch's brew.

MARGUERITE: It's just herbs and roots to strengthen the blood, Miz Joanne.

JOANNE: Don't talk to me about blood. I know. Thirteen pints and all of it white.

LOUELLA: Red, dear.

LOUELLA: Oh shut up!

LIZZIE: Well what with all this talk about black blood, white blood and hospitals, no one notices the moccasin snake sliding round the porch steps looking for a shady place in the cool.

JOANNE: Oh my god, I've been bitten!

LOUELLA: A snake, it's there, a snake!

LIZZIE: Quick as a flash of sunlight, Marguerite picks up the broom and shoosh sends the moccasin snake flying off the porch and into the bushes.

JOANNE: I'm going to die!

LOUELLA: Oh lord. Oh lord.

MARGUERITE: Stop waving your arm around. You make the poison travel.

LIZZIE: And Marguerite puts the cut to her mouth and sucks hard. And spits out the poison, blood and all.

JOANNE: Savage!

LIZZIE: Marguerite rips a piece off of Miz Joanne's skirt.

JOANNE: My dress!

LIZZIE: And ties it onto her arm.

JOANNE: Ouch, you're hurting. It's too tight.

MARGUERITE: Miz Louella, ma'am, get down off of that chair and hold her arm real tight, just here. Don't loosen up.

JOANNE: She drank my blood.

MARGUERITE: Just as likely to be mine, Miz Joanne ma'am. I been giving blood down that hospital since I been grown. And only label on the bottles is the blood group.

JOANNE: Oh my God, black blood!

LIZZIE: Marguerite got one more thing to say before she leave and don't come back.

MARGUERITE: You lie still while I wash my mouth. I sucked most of the snake poison out I think, but seems like you making your own poison right inside your head. Next time you get bitten, I reckon it's the snake going to need treatment. Goodbye.

Song: 'Little David Play On Your Harp'.

Scene Three

MAMA *and* MARGUERITE *are doing*

the washing in the same tub as LIZZIE *was bathed in.* LIZZIE *runs on waving an airmail letter.*

LIZZIE: Mama! It's a letter! From Charles!

MAMA: Is that so?

MARGUERITE: Aren't you going to open it?

MAMA *wipes her hands carefully.*

MAMA: In my own time.

LIZZIE: You going to read it to us too?

MAMA: You carry on with that washing.

LIZZIE *hangs out the washing.*

Dear Mama, How are you? I am OK I guess. Remember Joshua Regan, enlisted same time as me? He went kinda crazy a while back and they're shipping him home today. Hope this reaches you. It seems a real long way away. The officers tell us we're winning, so I guess we are. Yesterday we entered the city, I'm not allowed to say which one. We followed the bombing our boys done from the air. They done a good job it's said, near flattened it. As we went in I saw a girl, 'bout Lizzie's age I guess, trapped in the rubble from the waist down. She was singing while they tried to dig her out. I stayed there. They told me she said she could feel with her feet the corpses of her parents. And still she kept on singing. She had short black hair and skinny yellow brown arms. She died this morning. I don't know which side she was on. It's very hot. They don't have Thanksgiving here, so no turkey. Your loving son, Charles. P.S. Her name was Miko.'

Go fill up the can, Marguerite. Time to water the garden.

MARGUERITE *exits whistling 'John Brown's Body' softly.*

LIZZIE: Whenever Mama felt real bad we'd go to church. Like our people done since time began we'd sing our tears and our hopes.

Scene Four

Church. MAMA, LIZZIE *and* MARGUERITE *are there.*
The PREACHER *enters.*

PREACHER: I will now call upon Lizzie Walker to lead the sisters and brothers in the singing of 'Swing Low Sweet Chariot'.

LIZZIE: During slavery all that Swing Low Sweet Chariot coming for to carry me home, wasn't about dying like the white folks thought. It meant, tonight we makes a break for it. Kinda code, Mama says.

LIZZIE *sings 'Swing Low' alone.*

PREACHER: Thank you, Lizzie. And the Lord said, 'Let my people go. And if you refuse to let them go behold I will smite all thy borders with frogs.'

LIZZIE *starts to write a list.*

LIZZIE: Frogs.

PREACHER: And the Lord did it. And Pharaoh said, 'Verily Lord, I will let them go.' But he lied and did not free the people of Israel. So the Lord brought down a plague of lice and great swarms of flies and a plague of boils.

LIZZIE: Boils? Euch!

PREACHER: And yet and still Pharaoh lied and would not set my people free. And the Lord sent thunder and hail and the fire ran along upon the ground and there was darkness over the land of Egypt, even darkness which may be felt.

LIZZIE: Marguerite.

MARGUERITE: Ssh.

LIZZIE: But listen . . .

PREACHER: And he sent a plague of locusts and finally the Lord caused the firstborn children to die. Lord, let my people go!

MAMA: Amen!

PREACHER: And now let us speak with the Lord.

They pray. LIZZIE *continues writing her list.*

LIZZIE: Locusts.

MARGUERITE: What you writing Lizzie?

LIZZIE: It's a list.

MARGUERITE: What for?

LIZZIE: I'm working out when we're going to be free.

MARGUERITE: What are you talking about?

LIZZIE: Well, we had the hailstorm Monday, flies and frogs we got a plenty, three in our class got head lice and Mrs Jameson's eldest, Joby, got killed overseas and he had boils.

MARGUERITE: You're crazy!

LIZZIE: On the back of his neck. So I reckon can't be long now. Just waiting on the locusts.

The PREACHER *shakes hands at the door.*

PREACHER: Good day, Mrs Walker.

MAMA: Good day, Reverend.

PREACHER: Good day, Lizzie.

LIZZIE: Will be soon as we spot a locust.

PREACHER: Pardon me?

MARGUERITE: She don't mean nothing, sir. Good day, sir.

PREACHER: Good day, Marguerite.

The PREACHER *exits.*

LIZZIE: I do so too.

MARGUERITE: It was a plague of locusts, not one!

LIZZIE: Well Mama says I'm a plague and there's only one of me. So soon as I see just one locust my list'll be complete.

MAMA: Marguerite, Lizzie, come on now.

LIZZIE: Marguerite give up arguing with me then and there. I didn't let on a while later that I read about John the Baptist in the wilderness living on wild honey and locusts. I mean, how we going to get free if the folks supposed to be on our side keeps eating up the locusts?

Two verses of 'Little David'.

Scene Five

LIZZIE *is standing on a stool while* MAMA *alters the hem on one of* MARGUERITE *or* CHARLES' *handmedowns.*

MAMA: And she raised herself up in front of this crowd of heckling hostile folks and she fixed them with a look and she said:

SOJOURNER: Children, I have come here like the rest of you to hear what I have to say. I've heard tell you'll set fire to the building if a black woman gets to speak. Go ahead if you've a mind. I'll speak on the ashes if necessary. When I was a slave away down there in New York there was some particularly bad work to be done some coloured woman was sure to be called on to do it and when I hear that man talking about my people as nearer to animals and only useful as slaves I said to myself – this is the job for me. I am pure African, not one drop of white blood in me and that makes me real proud. The way you white folks behaving you ain't got no cause to be proud.

MAMA: And a voice from the crowd shouted:

WHITE HECKLER: Listen to that storm blowing out there. It is God's wrath come to strike this meeting!

SOJOURNER: Child, don't be scared. You are not going to be harmed. I don't expect God's ever heard tell of you.

MAMA: That didn't quiet him.

WHITE HECKLER: Old woman, do you think your talk of slavery does any good? Why, I don't care any more for your talk than I do for the bite of a flea!

SOJOURNER: Perhaps not, but the Lord willing, I'll keep you scratching.

MAMA: That Sojourner had the measure of him all right.

WHITE HECKLER: We already have a Constitution says 'all men are equal'. So why you going on about rights?

SOJOURNER: Now I hear talk about this Constitution and the right of man. I come up and take hold of this Constitution. It looks mighty big. And I feel for my rights. But they aren't there. Then I say to God, 'God, what ails this Constitution?' and you know what he says to me? God says, 'Sojourner, there's a little weevil in it.'

MAMA: And the thing about weevils is – they very hard to get rid of. Wheat looks fine till you crack it open and looks inside. Then you find the heart eaten out. Now I tell you child, beware of folk with their hearts eaten out. All done.

LIZZIE *climbs off the stool and starts to unpick the old seams of the garment* MAMA *pinned.*

LIZZIE: Now there's several ways to eat out the heart. Take the movies. Me, I used to save up pennies and go every chance I had. Hollywood, California, Sunset Strip – these were powerful magical words conjuring up for me how the world outside our town was. I told Marguerite about it when I got home. She was still out of a job and had taken to going out alone all of a sudden and coming back with bundles hid under her sweater. She was getting awful secretive and if there's one thing I can't abide it's secrets.

Scene Six

LIZZIE *is practising tap dancing like the movies.*

LIZZIE: Hi Marguerite.

MARGUERITE: Hi.

LIZZIE: You been someplace nice?

MARGUERITE: Mn.

LIZZIE: Sky fell in just afore dinnertime.

MARGUERITE: Oh yea.

LIZZIE: Thirty people injured by falling stars.

MARGUERITE: Really.

LIZZIE: It's like talking to Adam. I'm not keen on snakes though so I keep on trying. What you got under your sweater Marguerite?

MARGUERITE: Nothing.

LIZZIE: Well in that case if I was you I'd get on down see the doctor real fast cos you got a bump developing in the wrong place, sister.

MARGUERITE: That so?

MARGUERITE *opens the tin trunk, slithers something inside and locks it again.*

LIZZIE: Hey Marguerite, where d'you find a turtle with no legs?

MARGUERITE: I don't know.

LIZZIE: Where you left it.

No response.

Where you left it, get it?

You know Marguerite, I saw this movie and I reckon I know why you can't get a job. See, all the black folks in the movies who wait on table, are housemaids and all, well even in the old days, they smile.

And when they ain't waiting on tables smiling, they dancing and smiling. They never stop smiling. Like they advertising toothpaste dawn to dusk. Don't know how they eat their food wearing those big grins – but they don't show you that part. Must be kinda difficult. But if you practised in front of the mirror I'm sure you could learn it.

MARGUERITE: What!

LIZZIE: I should have seen the weather signs but I just ploughed on in. Today I saw this one about Al Jolson. He sings our songs and there was this one Mama would have liked real well – all about his mother.

LIZZIE *tap dances and sings, minstrel-style: 'Mammee'. She is really enjoying herself.*

MARGUERITE: Shut up.

LIZZIE: And there was me thinking I had a future in show business.

MARGUERITE: Don't you ever sing that song.

LIZZIE: What's the matter with you?

MARGUERITE: You ever hear your mother called 'Mammee?'

LIZZIE: No but . . .

MARGUERITE: You ever heard any black folks singing that song?

LIZZIE: Well no, but . . .

MARGUERITE: 'Swannee River'?

LIZZIE: You seen the movie! Why didn't you say so?

MARGUERITE: I seen some white guy blacking his face, making up songs about the brothers and sisters. What he know about being black? He's just making money off of our backs.

LIZZIE: It's only a movie.

MARGUERITE: And the way they tell it, you only some happy grinning nigger!

LIZZIE: Come to think on it, not only did I not know one woman answering to the name of 'Mammee', but I couldn't recall anyone I'd met smiling that much neither – particularly when they cleaning up someone else's mess. Marguerite?

MARGUERITE: Yes.

LIZZIE: Do they have a lot of black folks in Hollywood, you know, like producers an directors and all?

MARGUERITE: What do you think, dummy?

LIZZIE (*to the audience*): Dummy huh?

When they make us look foolish it's to keep us under and make them look smart, right?

MARGUERITE: Right.

LIZZIE: They shouldn't do that, should they?

MARGUERITE: No, they shouldn't.

LIZZIE: And the only way we can find out and tell it like it is, is to ask, right?

MARGUERITE: Of course.

LIZZIE: And brothers and sisters should be treated with respect.

MARGUERITE: That's right, yes.

LIZZIE: In that case I don't think you ought to call me dummy, and what you got in that box?

MARGUERITE: Corpses.

LIZZIE: What?

MARGUERITE: Corpses.

LIZZIE: Real live corpses?

MARGUERITE: Corpses.

MARGUERITE *exits.*

LIZZIE: Well, I just contemplating whether to have one of the fainting fits I hear tell white folks so good at. Perhaps my sister taken to murdering awful small people. I feel the spring coiling tighter and all of a sudden I could hear the dogs of evil snapping at our heels, they slipped their chains and running lose. Somebody going to get bit. Top it all, Mama comes in yelling . . .

MAMA: You forgot to feed the chickens!

Song: 'Hush You Bye', hummed through this next speech and then sung at the end.

LIZZIE: And it wasn't even my turn! Outside I made toe patterns in the dust, wondering why I'm always the one getting hollered at. Stayed out there, thinking about running away, till the mockingbird stopped calling, dark was wrapping all around me, and it didn't seem like such a good idea. Maybe I'd go some other time instead.

Scene Seven

The yard. LIZZIE *is sitting over an essay, chewing her pencil.* MAMA *is sweeping.*

LIZZIE: One hot day I was sitting in the yard trying to figure out how to write this essay we'd been given in school. It had a real dumb title: 'My favourite animal'. Well, I didn't have no favourite animal. I didn't mind pigs – they useful garbage disposal sort of creatures, but you can't hug a pig. I was finding it real hard to come up with an animal I could bear writing about when I realised Mama been talking to me.

MAMA: What's the matter, Lizzie, cat got your tongue?

LIZZIE: Cats? Now that's a possibility.

MAMA: You want to know more about cats you should go see Uncle Chrystal. He been training cats long as I can recall.

MAMA *laughs and leaves.*

Scene Eight

LIZZIE: Now my Great Uncle Chrystal was about 200 years old, well anyways he been around for a long time. His full name was Chrystal Obediah Diamond. Some folks said my Great Aunt Esther only married him on account of his fancy name. It did suit him real well cos even now he was so old and crêpey his eyes sort of glittered, specially when he got onto the subject of the code for training cats.

UNCLE CHRYSTAL *enters and sits with a feather duster and a rubber mouse.*

UNCLE: OK Esther, you get that mouse now. Go get him!

He thwacks thin air with the duster.

LIZZIE: Ever since Great Aunt Esther died all Uncle Chrystal's cats were called Esther.
Afternoon, Uncle Chrystal.

UNCLE: Who's that?

LIZZIE: It's me. Lizzie.

UNCLE: Nice to see you, child. Sit yourself down. Mind out for Esther. She's in training.

LIZZIE: Nice to see you, was just a way of talking. Uncle Chrystal was near blind as an owl at midday. How's it going, sir?

UNCLE: Well you got to keep to the code, child. I put down the mouse and wriggles the duster near it so old Esther thinks it's moving and then she pounces. And if she carry on lying in the sun and take no notice I thwacks her a blow with the feathers. Like so! Move it, Esther!

LIZZIE: Every now and then Esther would come up to the porch for a stroke or some food, Uncle would hit her over the head with the feather duster and she'd wander off looking kinda dazed. But mostly she kept clear and chased blue jays.

UNCLE: Move it, Esther!

LIZZIE: I guess she was trying to get her own back on the feathers. Uncle Chrystal?

UNCLE: Who's that?

LIZZIE: It's me, Lizzie.

UNCLE: That's funny. I had a great-neice called Lizzie once.

LIZZIE: Yea, that's me.

UNCLE: You sure?

LIZZIE: I come to ask about your code for training cats.

UNCLE: That's right.

LIZZIE: Well, does it work?

UNCLE: When they obey it does.

LIZZIE: And when they don't?

UNCLE: You hit em. Whack!

LIZZIE: Is a code sort of like a law, sir?

UNCLE: Yes, child. There's good codes and bad codes. And some just goes on going on account of no one shouts loud enough that they wrong.

LIZZIE: How d'you know what to shout?

UNCLE: Well, Esther used to say, on certain nights if you stamp hard enough, shout loud enough and sing home, you can hear the ancestral bones speak their speak. I guess that's how you know. Esther?

LIZZIE: Why all your cats called Esther anyways?

UNCLE: What?

LIZZIE: The name, Esther?

UNCLE: Always been an Esther in the family. Passed the name on down. Now my wife, her granma was an Esther too, from Africa. And she got dealt with by a code.

LIZZIE: What sort of a code, Uncle?

UNCLE: Well more of a law I guess. The English who in the business of stealing your African ancestors and selling them for slaves invented it. It sort of got passed on too.

LIZZIE: But what happened to Esther?

UNCLE: One day her master say he selling her daughter away to another plantation.

LIZZIE: Yea, and?

UNCLE: Well, this Esther she say no, this child all I got left of family now. So he beat her like a dog.

LIZZIE: What happened?

UNCLE: She died, child.

LIZZIE: Did they lock him up?

UNCLE: What for? He own her. He can do what he like.

LIZZIE: But she's a person!

UNCLE: Uh uh. She his property.

LIZZIE: That ain't right.

UNCLE: It the law though. Law say 'Christians will not be punished for destroying what belongs to them'. He bought her. She his.

LIZZIE: Christians?

UNCLE: They meant white folks.

LIZZIE: But black folks are Christians too.

UNCLE: Depends on who's owning God at the time, child. You seen that cat?

LIZZIE: She's in the bushes, back of the yard someplace.

UNCLE: You sure?

LIZZIE: Well, I can't see her.

UNCLE: You know sometimes I have this dream all the Esthers get together and come back, take over my place. And they learned to use the can opener so they gets their own food. Then they lies on my body, so many I just breath out from their weight and never breathes in again. Don't know why I dream that cos I never once let an Esther sleep on the bed.

LIZZIE: Maybe your code for training cats isn't too good, Uncle Chrystal.

UNCLE: She's my cat! I own her and I do what I like!

LIZZIE: As I left, Uncle Chrystal was dozing on the porch, his stick with the feathers still in his hand. Struck me, just cos you're old doesn't mean you know everything, not bone-deep anyhow. I went round the back of the yard looking for old Esther. There she was, nose deep in a petunia. She look up, pollen on her whiskers like face powder. She wasn't smiling neither. All the dusty road home I shouted and I stamped and I sang till the ancestral bones spoke their speak.

Last verse 'Little David'.

Scene Nine

It is another day. MARGUERITE is about to go out. LIZZIE is sitting in the kitchen.

LIZZIE: Where you going, Marguerite?

MARGUERITE: Out.

LIZZIE: Sometimes sisters are such a pain. Where out?

MARGUERITE: Downtown.

MARGUERITE *puts on her scarf from the costume trunk.*

LIZZIE: What to do?

MARGUERITE: March.

LIZZIE: Oh that.

MARGUERITE: You want to come too?

LIZZIE: Uh uh!

MARGUERITE: Bye then.

LIZZIE: Bye.

MARGUERITE *exits.*

Hey Marguerite, why you put on your best scarf? You going to meet some boy on that march? You going to do kissing and all that stuff are you? Are you?

No reply.

No fun teasing some folks. What to do with Marguerite gone. No one to pester. I decides to daydream instead.

LIZZIE *turns on the radio, a local station playing Billie Holiday.*

Must have been a good coupla hours later I come to and what did I see sitting there in front of me? The key! That's what. The key to Marguerite's tin trunk!

LIZZIE *looks around and goes to the trunk.* MAMA's *voice is heard off.*

MAMA: Lizzie, you done your schoolwork yet?

LIZZIE: Yes, Mama.

MAMA: What you doing then?

LIZZIE: Nothing much, Mama. (*To herself*:) Just finding out about corpses.

As LIZZIE *unlocks and opens the trunk a newsflash comes on the radio.*

NEWSCASTER: We interrupt this programme to bring you a newsflash. Disturbances have again hit the downtown area as protesters marched on City Hall. Police report rioting broke out during the march and injuries have been sustained on both sides.

During the above LIZZIE *starts to pay attention. Though she has seen the contents of the trunk she closes the lid.*

LIZZIE: The sharp crack of bullet hitting bone sped along the street, past the marchers fleeing in all directions, echoed through the empty corridors of City Hall, dodged through the grey green of the swamp, leapt the river, wove along the dirt track, round the corner of the porch, and slid under the kitchen door and into my ears. I knew. Marguerite! No! Marguerite!

During the following speech MARGUERITE *appears on stage and mimes the actions. At the sound of the shot she leaves. 'She Know Moon-rise' is hummed.*

Her friends say she was happy that day. Smiling. As they marched and sang she danced, waving her banner. She was near the front of the marchers. The police fired three tear-gas bombs, even though there was no trouble. And my sister picked one up and threw it back at them. She was no rioter. That moment she was just angry. She threw the gas back and they shot her, and others too. Her friends say she was very tall that day, like her great-great-grandma some say.

Song: last verse of 'She Know Moon-rise'. LIZZIE, *running. Her way is blocked by the cop.*

No! Let me through! I want my sister! Marguerite! What have you done with her?

COP: Move back! Get this kid outa here!

LIZZIE: I want my sister. You have no right!

LIZZIE *raises her arm. The* COP *grabs it and twists it.*

COP: Halt!

The COP *leaves.*

LIZZIE: Mama bailed me out of gaol the next morning. They let me go but they would not give up Marguerite's body. She was locked in the City Morgue awaiting a post-mortem, they said. That's when they cut up the dead body to see whose fault it was. I could have told them.

Scene Ten

LIZZIE *paces in circles.* MAMA *enters. It is night in the kitchen.*

MAMA: Child, you must get some rest.

LIZZIE: Not until she's buried.

MAMA: It been five nights now, Lizzie honey. You going to get sick.

LIZZIE: She ought to be buried.

MAMA: Lizzie, child, let it rest now.

LIZZIE: Not until she does. It just not right.

MAMA: Ain't there enough sorrow in this house!

LIZZIE: Mama, I can't sleep. I don't rightly know what to do. I got to figure it out.

MAMA: Marguerite, my baby, she still here with us now, like the other sisters.

LIZZIE: No she aint! She still in a metal drawer in the City Morgue. She's dead but they still holding her prisoner!

MAMA: Child, please. No more.

LIZZIE: Mama, was you taught me my history.

MAMA: That was a long time ago. Lifetime ago.

LIZZIE: No! Tell me again what Sojourner say, Mama.

MAMA: I'm all tired out, Lizzie. The misery's in my bones now, Lord knows.

LIZZIE: You tell me Sojourner say 'If women want any rights' . . .

MAMA: No, just rest. Just tonight.

LIZZIE: 'If women want any rights more than they got, why don't they just take them and not be talking about it?' Ain't that the truth, Mama?

MAMA: You the only one I got left.

LIZZIE: I know. I'm sorry. Go back to bed, Mama.

MAMA: I'll sit up with you.

LIZZIE: All right.

MAMA: Where I can see you.

LIZZIE (*covering* MAMA): Go to sleep.

LIZZIE *watches* MAMA *nodding in the chair, covered with the half-finished quilt, and speaks to herself as she quietly leaves.*

Why don't they just take them?

Scene Eleven

As MAMA *sleeps in the chair the sound of* two white women *talking.*

FIRST WOMAN: Did you hear?

SECOND WOMAN: Did you hear?

FIRST WOMAN: The rioting.

SECOND WOMAN: Dreadful. Blacks.

FIRST WOMAN: Looting.

SECOND WOMAN: Burning.

FIRST WOMAN: Shooting.

SECOND WOMAN: Law and order.

FIRST WOMAN: Getting uppity.

SECOND WOMAN: Wanting rights.

FIRST WOMAN: Control.

SECOND WOMAN: Police.

FIRST WOMAN: Law.

SECOND WOMAN: Order.

FIRST WOMAN: Did you hear?

SECOND WOMAN: Did you hear?

FIRST WOMAN: Body stolen.

SECOND WOMAN: Break in.

FIRST WOMAN: At dawn.

SECOND WOMAN: Bold as you like.

FIRST WOMAN: City Morgue.

SECOND WOMAN: Black body.

FIRST WOMAN: Rioter.

SECOND WOMAN: And a woman.

FIRST WOMAN: Not proper.

SECOND WOMAN: Outrageous.

FIRST WOMAN: Learn their place.

SECOND WOMAN: Learn their place.

Scene Twelve

MAMA *wakes stiffly.*

MAMA: Ouch. I too old for this sitting up sleeping game. Lizzie. Lizzie?

LIZZIE *enters.*

LIZZIE: Here, Mama.

MAMA: Child, you look like ghosts got you. What you been doing?

LIZZIE: Could I have a cup of milk, I'm real tired, Mama.

MAMA: Course, child.

LIZZIE: I been to get Marguerite. I been to get my sister.

MAMA: What!

LIZZIE: I said . . .

MAMA: I hear what you said. Are you crazy? Are you telling me you broke into the morgue and stole your sister's body?

LIZZIE: How could I 'steal' my own sister?

MAMA: How'd you get in? That place locked solid.

LIZZIE: Charles pass on to me some of the skills the army taught him.

MAMA: Did anyone see you? Lord you going to be in big trouble if they did.

LIZZIE: Mama, they ain't that stupid. Trouble's my middle name now I reckon.

MAMA: They going to arrest you.

LIZZIE: I know. Let them.

MAMA: Tell me, child.

LIZZIE: Harriet died alone selling vegetables on the street. History books forgot Sojourner. They threw my great-granma's bones in the yard. My sister going to be treated with respect. She going to be buried proper. And all this stuff along with her.

MAMA: What's that?

LIZZIE: Marguerite called them corpses. It's ornaments she took from white folks' houses, from shops and art stores – black boys holding up lamps, bookends made like black women, toasting forks with black grinning faces on their handles. They going to be buried too. We ain't things. We people.

LIZZIE *and* MAMA *move the trunk.*

MAMA: It's heavy.

LIZZIE: It would be.

MAMA: Lizzie, stand up a moment.

LIZZIE *does so.*

You grown. You getting to be real tall – just like . . .

Song: One verse of 'Let My People Go'.

LIZZIE: I had a great-great-granma. She took Sojourner Truth as her name. I am her great-great-granddaughter. I am Marguerite's sister. I am Mama's daughter. I am Lizzie Walker taking the name of Trouble because of the trouble behind, taking the name of Fighter because of the struggle ahead. I am Lizzie Walker, on my own story, walking my own road. But we treading it together, sisters. Been walked before. Be walked again.

Song: reprise 'No More Moaning', up tempo.

Stamping, Shouting and Singing Home

About two years prior to my being commissioned by Watford to write *Stamping, Shouting and Singing Home*, Gwenda Hughes rang me to say, 'I've found this speech by a black American woman called Sojourner Truth. It's called "Ain't I a Woman?" and she's a heroine. We should do a play about her.' Two years on the company was addressing the educative needs of its audience, i.e. young people, and one of the large gaps appeared to be the lack of black history and in particular the history of black women. They decided it was time for Sojourner Truth and Harriet Tubman, her sister in America, to take the stage.

Alice Walker has long been one of my heroines and I am indebted to her work, and to that of writers such as Maya Angelou, Toni Cade Bambara, Toni Morrison, Rosa Guy and, in contrast, to that of Harriet Beecher Stowe. In England it proved impossible to find any but the scantiest references to Sojourner Truth, but as I had lived and worked in America, I sent to friends there who posted American publications on both Sojourner and Harriet to me.

I listened to African and Afro-Caribbean story-tellers, as the oral tradition of handing on history seemed an important part of the patchwork of the play. The songs had to be there too. To oppressed people the world over they have their own language, of courage, solace and information.

The play was originally conceived and written for an audience of 9-13-year-olds but in both its original and subsequent productions it played to audiences of all ages.

Despite woefully inadequate funding the production was of an extremely high standard and the company deservedly received much praise. Since then the play has had three further productions and in 1987 I wrote a radio version which went out as a Monday Night Play on Radio 4 the same year.

Lisa Evans started in theatre as a performer, working both in Britain and in the USA. In 1979, while at the National Theatre, she started writing, and her first play, *Ring O' Roses*, was accepted by the BBC and broadcast in 1981. This was closely followed by a production at the Soho Poly Theatre, London, of her first stage play, *Mother's Day*, about a daughter arriving home, pregnant, on Mother's Day. Her other stage plays include *Inside Out*, about a single parent sent to prison for a petty offence, *Face Values*, set in Kent in the summer of 1983 and focusing on the women involved in the mining dispute; *Taking Liberties*, about two nineteenth-century working-class northern families who win a lottery and move to a Chartist farm in the south (1985); *Crime of the Century*, a play set in rural Suffolk at the time of Captain Swing and the uprisings of the 1820s and 1830s (1986); *Under Exposure,* about women in Crossroads squatter camp, South Africa; and *Better than Burning*, the story of three generations of a Punjabi family living in Britain (1987).

NIGHT
(L'HOMME GRIS)

Marie Laberge
Translated by Rina Fraticelli

Characters

Roland Fréchette, *52, Christine's father*
The very picture of a man of goodwill. Not a very large man; rather thin, well groomed, paying great attention to his physical appearance. He is a confident man, sure of himself and of his opinions, one who never doubts for an instant the moral rightness of his actions. He long ago denied the world of emotions: this he considers to be a good thing, as he's felt a lot better for it. As a result, he is thoroughly incapable of appreciating what his daughter is feeling.

Christine, *21 years old*
Extremely slight, thin. She is the incarnation of deeply internalised anxiety. In contrast with her father, she is thin-skinned and highly sensitive. Every minor nuance and vague implication of her father's words resonates loudly for her. And there are wounds . . .. Her very presence (without any need to overstate the acting) should help us gauge her father's words. She was once anorexic.

L'Homme Gris was first produced in Montreal on 13 September 1984 by Les Productions Marie Laberge and Le Théâtre du Vieux Québec, with the following cast:

ROLAND FRÉCHETTE   Yvon Leroux
CHRISTINE   Marie Michaud

Directed by Marie Laberge
Set and lighting design by Pierre Labonté
Costumes by Carole Paré

This production was remounted in Québec city on 26 March 1985 at l'Implanthéâtre, with Marc Legault as ROLAND FRÉCHETTE and Marie Michaud as CHRISTINE.

The English-language première of *L'Homme gris/Night* was produced by Toronto Free Theatre on 2 March 1988, with the following cast:

ROLAND FRÉCHETTE   David Fox
CHRISTINE   Karen Woolridge

Directed by Richard Greenblatt
Set and costumes designed by Jules Tonus
Lighting designed by Jim Plaxton
Fight direction by Robert Lindsay
Stage Manager Winston Morgan

For Micheline Bernard

He waited for the black, terrible anger as though for some beast out of the night. But it did not come to him. His bowels seemed weighted with lead, and he walked slowly and lingered against fences and the cold, wet walls of buildings by the way. Descent into the depths until at last there was no further chasm below. He touched the solid bottom of despair and there took ease.

(Carson McCullers, The Heart is a Lonely Hunter)

A motel. Typical, conventional, boring and cheap. Twin beds separated by a night-table on which sits the telephone and a single large and ugly lamp. Stage left, a door and a window onto the outside. Stage right, the doors to the closet and to the bathroom. Downstage are a low table which will be used for the meal, and two so-called comfortable chairs, odds and ends which might have come from a living-room circa 1960, the colours of all of which clash. In terms of the colours, what's most important is that they be more or less worn out while retaining a quality of harshness: carpets whose patterns are old and worn but none the less abrasive; garish bedspreads; lamps and curtains of extremely questionable taste. Finally, a multidirectional television set which, at the opening, is positioned toward the beds.

At the opening, the stage is lit exclusively by the glow of the motel sign, reflected through the window. As the door opens, a narrow shaft of light streaks in. We hear the rain and a terrible thunderstorm. A man enters quickly. He drops an overnight bag by the door. In his other hand, he carries, very much at arm's length, two cardboard boxes tied together. He shakes the rain off himself, while taking in the room. He deposits the boxes on the table and turns back to the door. No one has followed him.

ROLAND: Chris! Hurry up! Get in here before you get soaked.

He goes to pick up the overnight bag by the door. CHRISTINE enters. She looks even younger than her age. Her hair is wet; her hands are stuck in the pockets of her navy, three-quarter-length trench coat; and she's wearing sneakers on her wet feet. She appears very uneasy. She comes in and stands stock-still in front of the window, by the TV, without showing the slightest interest in the motel room. (She ought to inspire in us the urge to gather her up, to comfort her, rock her.) ROLAND closes the door, deposits the overnight bag by the TV and switches on the overhead light which gives off a harsh, offensive glare.

Jesus! That's what you call a light! Just hang on a sec and I'll fix that up.

He springs back into action, full of cheer, somewhat strained in his high spirits. He turns on the bedside lamp, moving the table a little while he's at it, then the bathroom light, leaving the door ajar. The turning on of each light is punctuated by a satisfied 'All right!' CHRISTINE has not stirred. She drips quietly. ROLAND returns, turns off the overhead light and is satisfied.

All right! That's more like it. See, we just saved ourselves seven bucks, easy: it already looks more like a high-class motel. (*He goes over to the table and unties the boxes.*) Not bad for eighteen bucks! There's even a colour TV. Is it colour? Hang on a sec. (*He goes to check.*) Darn right, it's colour, Chris, a real first-class motel. Later on, we can watch a nice movie. (*He looks at her. She hasn't moved.*) Well, sit down, Chris. Take off your coat. We'll have some supper. That'll pick you right up, you'll see. (*He goes to get her, sits her down.*) Cold? Want me to turn up the heat? There's bound to be a thermostat in here somewhere.

He moves behind her to help her off with her coat. She resists, silently. He pats her shoulders, laughing but annoyed.

All right, all right, hang on to your coat. I'm not gonna force you. You're just like Mom, hmm, always shivering, just like Mom. Well, if it's all the same to you I'll just peel off a layer.

He takes off his trench coat and hangs it in the closet.

You'll be doing the same thing, before you know it, just wait and see.

Pause. He looks at her. He is still standing behind her. He is uneasy, a little uncomfortable. The good cheer is beginning to show signs of strain. Then, he finds a solution.

Well, now. I'd say I've earned a little drink. Will you have one, Chris? With lots and lots of water.

CHRISTINE *reacts for the first time. Alarmed, she watches him as he goes to his suitcase, opens it, taking out an unopened 26-ouncer of gin. He goes into the bathroom. We hear the glass,*

*water. He returns with a full glass for
himself and one considerably less full
for her. As soon as he enters the
bathroom, he starts talking louder.*

Don't get yourself into a state on
Mom's account. The fact that I
stopped just proves she's not dying.
You know perfectly well I'd have gone
straight home – I mean, to the hospital
if there was really any reason to
worry. Oh, it's serious, all right, but
like the doctors said, she's on the road
to recovery. We'll bring her through it.
(*He comes back into the room.*) Here.
Drink this up. It'll put a little colour in
your cheeks.

*He puts her glass on the table. She
doesn't touch it. Turning his back to
his daughter, facing the window, he
takes a long slug of his own.*

Talk about ugly weather. It hasn't let
up all day. When I left Sherbrooke,
I'm not kidding, I could've really used
a second set of wipers. Give me snow
over that kind of rain any day. First of
all, it's nicer to look at; and secondly,
it's cleaner. Don't talk to me about
rain like this in November.

*He finishes his drink in one gulp.
Clicks his tongue with satisfaction.*

That's a nice little drink.

*He turns back toward her; she hasn't
moved. He catches her biting her
nails.*

Are you hungry yet, Chris? We'll have
ourselves a fine little feast, you'll see.
(*He opens the boxes of barbecue
chicken.*) Aw, look at that. The
coleslaw went and spilled all over the
fries. No problem. Just hand that one
over to me. I'll eat it myself. There
you go, kiddo, enjoy!

*He pulls up an armchair and digs into
the chicken.* CHRISTINE *watches him
eat with considerable, one might even
say with a certain disgust. She returns
to biting her nails without having
touched her plate.*

Not bad. It's a little dry but the
coleslaw in the fries helps a little. Oh,
maybe I should've bought you a coke
to go with it, eh Chris?

He watches her chew her nails with

*some irritation. He obviously can't
stand it.*

Chris! Eat your chicken instead of
chewing your nails.

*She jumps, then quickly picks up a
piece of chicken, holding it gingerly in
her fingers.*

That's it. Be a good girl. I'll just go
and fix myself a little refill.

He exits to the bathroom.
CHRISTINE *drops the chicken and
begins to dry her fingers meticulously.
He returns.*

Not bad, is it? It's hard to go wrong
with chicken. Even Mom couldn't ruin
it. I said to myself, we'll get our
money's worth with chicken. And you
can eat it cold, no problem. Still and
all. They don't give it away. Two
boxes like this comes to just about 15
bucks with tax . . . bloody filthy tax.
They get us coming and going those
guys. And there's no end to it, kiddo.
They bleed you all the way to the
grave and then some. I give up trying
to figure out how to get past those
guys. I couldn't care less what the rich
have to pay. But people like us, when
you think how we started out, without
a cent, and now, just when we can
afford to relax a little, thanks to the
sweat and the sacrifices we made, you
know what I mean, well, it makes me
sick to watch them take away the little
bit extra we managed to put aside.
Like we weren't even entitled to a little
bit extra to make up for all the time
we did without. The old money, well,
they know every little trick and dodge
to keep from paying tax; it's easy for
them, they're practically born knowing
how to finagle their way around these
things. They didn't start playing kissy
face with the tax man just yesterday.
But a guy like me, who's just started
breathing a little easier in the last
couple of years . . .

CHRISTINE *takes her package of
cigarettes out of her pocket and is
about to take out a cigarette.*

You're not gonna smoke? You haven't
eaten a thing yet. No, no, eat a bit
more, then you can smoke. A person's
got to eat. (*He puts her cigarettes
aside, and watches her, waiting.*)

C'mon now, eat up. It's not poison, you'll see.

She picks up the same piece of chicken again, holding it gingerly in her fingers.

That's better. (*He goes back to work on his chicken voraciously.*) Mom's been really worried, always wondering if you were getting enough to eat. Well, you gotta admit, in Mom's case enough is a lot. At least as much as you and me combined. (*He laughs.*) I'm telling you nothing's changed on that score since you left. In fact, she's put on another fifteen pounds or so. and on top of what she already had to begin with, let me tell you, it shows. To think that when I married that woman she was as thin as you are right now. Unbelievable, hmm? Well, maybe a little more . . . filled out than you but not much. That's what you might call a 'distant memory'. I'm telling you, if we didn't have the wedding pictures, I'd have trouble believing it myself . . . . It was when you arrived that she put on the great bulk of it. It's like, after you, she never lost her pot . . . like she stayed pregnant even after you were born. Yeah, it was with you that she started to get fat. Seems like it's pretty hard, having a baby. (*He watches her, thoughtfully.*) I wonder if it'll have the same effect on you?

CHRISTINE *drops the chicken, barely touched; it's all she can do to keep from gagging.*

(*Angry:*) Not that it's likely, the way you eat. Do you eat at least? At home, I mean, with your husband, did you eat? You haven't started up that foolishness again, have you? It cost us enough, the pills and all . . . well, I certainly hope we've heard the last of that business.

He looks at her. She's biting her nails again. She stops abruptly, taken aback.

Is it just that you're worried about Mom? Don't be. Maybe I made it sound a little more serious than it actually is 'cause I wanted you to come back with me . . . Mom too . . . uh, this chicken's dry . . . .

He finishes his drink, and gets up to get another. As soon as he is in the bathroom CHRISTINE *takes out a cigarette.* ROLAND *enters.*

I think I can allow myself this one. Especially since we're not going back on the road tonight. I'm telling you, that was a long tough haul today. Worse still, in this weather . . . Mom was afraid it'd turn to snow . . . they were calling for freezing rain . . . well, I'm ready for any of it: four Michelin tyres.

The 'conversation' is running thin, he goes to the window.

No, it's not gonna freeze over; it's just gonna keep on raining. We're not going to be waking up to the first snow. Not tomorrow, anyway. so much the better or Mom'd have a fit. (*He comes around to the table again, his glass empty.*) You're not gonna eat your fries? Well, at least yours aren't soggy. Your coleslaw didn't spill into them. D'you mind if I steal a couple? (CHRISTINE *pushes the box across the table to him.*) Mine were a little too wet for my taste. Here, eat this little piece. (*He holds out a piece of chicken.*) Just this one and then I'll leave you alone about it. Be a good girl.

She chews at the chicken slowly while continuing to smoke.

Wouldn't you know it, your fries are better'n mine.

Time passes. He stops eating. Silence. He takes the wet napkin out of its pocket, wipes his fingers with it, and puts it back into the box on top of the chicken. He takes out his nail clippers and gives himself a little unnecessary touch up. Such endless trimming of his fingernails is one of ROLAND's *tics. A sigh.*

Yeah. Well, you're not a big talker, Chris. You never did make much noise, but this is something else again. Has marriage done this to you? (*He laughs a little, then stops abruptly.*) Maybe it's just that you take after me – talking doesn't come easy to you. Mom doesn't have that problem – she talks. You certainly don't feel time weighing on you, like, when she's around. That's one of her good points: she's good at making conversation. I wouldn't say she's always got the most important things to say but she talks, she fills the house, as they say. And especially since you left, she never stops yakking and fussing all the time. She's always off in a corner with one of the neighbours or else my sister, your aunt . . . cooking up something or other . . . well, it makes her happy and it doesn't bother anybody. Certainly doesn't bother me – I don't listen anymore! (*He laughs.*) It's like 'background noise', I mean like having a second TV going somewhere in the house . . . . But you, now, Chris, you never did say much of anything. Except when you were just little, you hardly ever made a sound in the house. That must mean you were happy . . . anyhow . . . we did everything so you would be . . . . We're not the kind who'd ever hurt you. And we never scrimped either . . . . All finished eating? Because there's something I want to talk to you about; I'd like to have a little talk with you. It's not something we've done much of, I know, but I think now . . . hmm . . . we don't have much choice . . . er . . . will you have another glass? Oh, no, you haven't even touched it . . . . Hold on a minute, I'll be right back.

He goes to refill his glass.
CHRISTINE, *extremely nervous, gnaws at her nails. He re-enters somewhat ill at ease, he doesn't know where or how to begin.*

You're thinking we could've gone straight home tonight, if I'd wanted to . . . I'd've been able to make it . . . . Well, I certainly didn't stop here just to throw good money out the window. No. I stopped because I needed to have a word with you before we got home, just the two of us. And it's not because anything bad's happened to Mom. No . . . uh . . . no . . . this morning, at your place when I told you about the heart attack . . . and the hospital . . . and Mom needing you with her and all – well, that wasn't exactly true. Let's say that . . . it was a kind of excuse I made up so I could get you out of your house and take you home. Do you understand?

She looks at him, dumbfounded, desperately chewing at a nail.

Will you *please* stop biting your bloody nails. It makes you look a real dummy. Do you understand what I'm saying to you? (*She indicates that she does and, trembling, lights a cigarette. He doesn't want to look at her anymore, begins to pace.*) Do I need to explain to you why I'm taking you back home?

She stares at him, like a trapped animal.

Jesus Christ! You'd think it was me you were afraid of. You don't need to be afraid of me, Chris, and you know it. What have I ever done to you? Nothing. Have I ever laid a finger on you? Ever hit you once? Never! I always managed to get myself out of the house before I really lost my temper. I always knew enough to get out of there before my hand got away from me. Same thing with Mom. Sometimes I wonder what good it ever did having all that control: it never stopped you from marrying a moron without even a decent trade. Anyhow, that's another story altogether. But you don't need to look at me with those big scared eyes – I never hurt you – I never touched you – and I'm not about to start today. Do you understand? Do you understand what I'm telling you?

She nods her head, rapidly, almost violently.

Jesus bloody Christ! – you're maddening! It's no wonder we want to grab you and shake something – a few words – anything – out of you once in a while. We wouldn't expect anything brilliant – don't worry!

He takes a swallow. Pause.

Ah . . . sorry. That's not what I wanted to say. I believe that you're real smart . . . anyway all the specialists we went to said so, you don't need to worry on that account. I even kept their written reports to prove it. It cost so much they had to give it to us in writing. At least you'll have them to make up for the diploma you never got. Don't get me wrong – I didn't say that to hurt you – I'm just telling you because someday it might be important to you. I kept all those papers just in case you need them, someday, to put your mind at ease, about yourself, like. (*Pause.*) But that's not what we were talking about, is it, eh, Chris? We were talking about Mom's heart attack; we were saying how it was a kind of excuse. (*Pause.*) I never lie, Chris, I've never told a lie in my entire life. You know perfectly well how I feel about lying. I can't stand it. As far as I'm concerned a liar is about the worst kind of person there is. Oh, I've had to stretch the truth a little on occasion – out of human kindness – I'll admit that – and I've been known to avoid a question – to say nothing at all, I mean, rather than be forced into a lie – that's how much it disgusts me, but today, this morning, I lied to you, and the worst of it is, is that it was you who forced me to lie. It's because of you that I lied. For you. I lied to you for your own good. Because if I'd've told you the real reason, you wouldn't've come back with me, you wouldn't've wanted to. And that's why, so I could tell my little lie – that Mom let me go alone. And that was a big deal for her, that was no small sacrifice. So now, in a little while, we'll call her, OK? We'll give her a call to put her mind at ease. And then she . . . can call your aunt. (*Pause.*) You know why I'm saying all this . . . don't you?

CHRISTINE *isn't smoking anymore. Her cigarette is simply burning itself out. She is stiff, frozen there in place.*

You just don't seem to understand, Chris . . .. When your aunt went to Rimouski to see you, three months ago, she figured out right away what was going on at your place. Seems like your idiot of a husband made no bones about letting her know what he thinks of her – and us too. I don't know if he drinks – if he has any excuse at all – all I know is that your aunt found him pretty bloody violent and she thought that you were looking pretty pitiful yourself, that you looked worn right out. So that – well – you know her – I mean – she doesn't waste any time – she stayed on in Rimouski two more days – in a hotel – all at her own expense – to do a little investigating. And the upshot of her investigation is that we found out all about it. Everything. Your aunt has her faults, God knows she exaggerates half the time, but with this, she even tried to hide some of the details from us – that's how shocked she was. She dug up her information about him, she talked to the people who live on your block – never letting on a thing, using all sorts of real-sounding reasons for asking. You know what a good liar she is. She convinced them she was thinking of moving into the building, just wanted to find out if it was peaceful or not . . . there's nothing she wouldn't't've said to get to the bottom of the story: and the bottom of the story is not very pretty. And when your aunt told me, well I wasn't very proud of you. She even told me – she didn't tell Mom this – but she told me that she saw you again, a little later – I guess she must've come up with another one of her lies – anyhow, she saw your sprained finger – 'accidentally' sprained like you told her. And that same day you were wearing a turtleneck sweater rolled practically up to your ears. And seems like everybody else was dying of heat. Did you actually think your aunt was gonna believe you? Did you actually think she was gonna buy your story about a cupboard door giving you a black eye? And what a good man your husband was? How understanding and kind he was being about your pain and all? What kind of suckers do you take us for, anyway? You're gonna have to come up with something a little better than that if you expect us to fall for it. You listen to me, Chris: there's no good reason for you to stay with him if he hits you; and there's no good reason for you to protect a guy like that. Did you ever once think of Mom? Forget about me, do you have any idea how ashamed Mom must have felt when your aunt told her? Do you have any idea how ashamed we'd be if something like this ever got out? I just don't understand how you can manage to love a guy like that – I mean, even before I knew he hit you, I couldn't understand – but now, well, I've got no choice . . . I've got to wonder if you're normal. Never – do you hear me – I'm never gonna let you go back to a guy that beats you. I'd rather live with the shame of divorce than risk someday somebody finding out about this. I'll never let anybody raise a hand to you. I never did it myself – and as long as I live I'll never let anybody else do it. And that's something you can count on, Chris: if you can't look after yourself – I don't care how old you are – I'll do it for you. Someone lays a hand on you – it's me they're hitting, me they're insulting, me they're cheapening. And I'm not about to be scared off by a little moron like your husband. Let him come and see me – he'll find out who he's doing business with. But he'll never lay a finger on me, that's for sure, or he'll be on the floor before he knows what hit him. But starting right now, you can just consider yourself divorced. It's not hard to plead physical cruelty in court. Never mind how much it costs, do you understand? I just don't know what you must have been thinking of to let yourself get beaten up like that for two years. I just hope it hasn't been going on for the whole two years. Because if it is two years, it's gonna take one helluva specialist to explain this one to me. You've got parents who love you. You could've come home any time, how many people can say that? We know where our duty lies – and we've never backed down from it, we always gave you the best of everything – whatever the cost – we never minded the sacrifices it meant. And all you can manage to do is get yourself beaten up by a stupid asshole who's barely five foot seven. You've got no pride, Chris, you got no pride – not for yourself and not for your parents . . . and don't you try telling me those lies you told your aunt, you know how . . .

CHRISTINE *begins to gag. She rushes into the bathroom and closes the door. Her father goes to the door, alarmed.*

Chris? Chris? Answer me. Are you sick? Are you throwing up? Do you need any help? Open the door, now, let me in! Chris?

Nothing but the sound of the toilet flushing.

Are you feeling better? Did that help? Are you feeling bad? Is that it? We won't talk about it anymore, if you don't want to. I understand it's hard for you. Open the door, now, Chris. You're not sick anymore, now, is it over? Come on. Come out of there, I'll take care of you. We won't talk about it anymore. Never. It's over. Dead and buried. We're gonna make a new life for you – you'll see. We'll only talk about it if you want to, if you need to. (*Pause.*) Are you feeling any better? Come on out of there, Chris . . .

CHRISTINE *comes out of the bathroom. She sits down at the edge of the bed.* ROLAND *rushes over to the table to remove the boxes.*

I'll just get rid of this. You don't need to have all this chicken staring you in the face. (*He gathers it all up quickly.*) Want me to turn on the TV? Maybe there's a nice movie on. It'd take your mind off things . . . just hang on a sec and I'll be right back.

His hands are full of boxes. He takes them to the trash can in the bathroom. He comes back, turns on the TV, puts the chairs back in place. She's still at the edge of the bed, frozen. He takes the glass he gave her.

Good thing you didn't drink it. It wouldn't've done you any good. (*He drinks it.*) You always did have a sensitive stomach, I mean, a kind of weakness in that area.

He sits in an armchair, takes out a cigarette and puts it in his mouth without lighting it.

Oh, don't worry, I'm not gonna light it. I'm trying to quit. It's a pretty good way, actually – all you have to do is not light it. It's almost the same thing: you just don't get the smoke.

No response. CHRISTINE *seems to have sunk into herself, beyond it all.*

Chris! Do you hear me? (*She starts, looks at him.*) Do you want one? You don't have to hold back on my account. (*She shakes her head slowly, her eyes full of tears.*) I'll stay right here . . . you can watch your programme, nice and peaceful. I'll finish up your drink . . . . (*He watches the movie for a bit.*) D'you want me to turn up the sound? I'll just turn up the sound a bit, we can't hear a thing.

He goes to turn up the sound. She's not listening to the TV. She's just sitting there, in despair. He sits down again, gets up again, gets his slippers out of his bag and puts them on. He sits back down. He goes over to turn out the bedside lamp. The soundtrack of the movie, a dialogue about love considerably different from what we've just been hearing, continues as the lights slowly dim.

The lights come up again after a little while, indicating time has passed. When they come up, CHRISTINE *is in the bathroom with the door closed;* ROLAND, *on his way to being, but not yet drunk, is on the telephone and nervous. He keeps a watch on the bathroom door.*

Yes. Collect, that's right . . .. Is that a problem? . . . Roland Frechette . . . uh huh . . .

He waits, drumming his fingers, fussing with the pillows on CHRISTINE's *bed. There is a response at the other end of the line.*

Say 'yes' Mom . . . Good . . . Yes, yes, it's me, it's me . . . No, we stopped on the way just like I said I'd do . . .. We're at Joly, now. Well, of course she's with me . . . All right, now listen, I can't talk too long but there's something I want to tell you: it's better if we don't say too much about it, d'you understand? Not a word about Frank and all that or the marriage or anything . . .. Well, of course! Enough to make her sick, she hasn't stopped running back and forth to the bathroom since we got here . . .. Stop screaming Mom, it's not that, it's just the shock.

CHRISTINE *comes out of the bathroom without making a sound. She's still wearing her coat. She leans against the door frame.* ROLAND *doesn't see her.*

Let's just hold on before we start jumping to conclusions, OK? Let's just say she's feeling sick . . . yeah, tomorrow morning early . . . It'll

depend on Chris, if she's sick all night . . ..

He turns around, sees her and pats the bed so she'll come and sit down, smiles in a discouraged sort of way as if to indicate that he's speaking to someone quite unreasonable.

OK . . . OK . . . I'll do that . . . fine . . . good . . . that's enough, now . . . this is long distance . . . that's right . . .. Goodnight, now. (*He hangs up.*) She's real worried. You know her, she always suspects the worst. If it was up to her we'd be on our way to emergency at Joly right now. And let me tell you I'm jolly well not driving way over there. (*He laughs.*) You OK? Are you still cold? Come and get yourself settled in over here. Don't keep hanging around the bathroom like that, it'll just give you ideas.

He goes to get her, she sits on the edge of the bed.

I've never known anyone who had such a weak stomach . . . you've been vomiting ever since you were twelve . . . Mom's not exactly wrong to worry . . . we figured all that vomiting was over and done with . . . we thought you'd finished with all that stuff . . .. As far as I'm concerned, you never saw the right specialist . . .. (*Pause.*) Maybe it's the flu, hmm? There's a lot of it around this time of year, and this one's a real mean bugger: one of my salesmen had it, he missed a week and a half of work and he was still green around the gills when he came back. I'm not kidding.

Pause. ROLAND *is at a loss. He walks around her.*

Chris, if you have the flu, you know, you ought to take off that wet coat; and your shoes too. Here I'll help you.

He moves as if to help her. She immediately shrinks away from him, wrapping her arms around herself.

No? You don't want to? I'm just telling you it'd help, it'd warm you up.

She pulls away abruptly in a protective move. He reacts as if attacked.

No? Suit yourself. I'm certainly not gonna coax you. Not like Mom does, that's for sure.

He gets his empty glass from the table and goes to the bathroom to refill it. CHRISTINE moves toward the very end of the bed; one might well imagine that she is in a competition for the person who can take up the least amount of space. She draws into herself and we see her becoming more and more anxious, but without the energy to defend herself, giving her the terrified look of someone poised on alert. Nevertheless she is attuned to and registers every word that's spoken. ROLAND re-enters with his glass. He's had a lot to drink but doesn't 'read' drunk in the conventional way. It's a highly internalized drunkenness that's reflected more in what he says than how he speaks.

You OK? D'you need anything? Too bad we don't have any pills or anything with us. If Mom was here, we'd have everything we need. Mom never leaves the house without her pills – she's like a preacher with his bible. (*He laughs. Pause. He sits on the chair.*) No, it's no joke to be stuck like this . . . I just hope you can get a little sleep. If not, Mom's gonna think I've been beating up on you, too.

He realises abruptly what he's just said, and looks at her.

Oh, sorry, it's just an expression . . . (*Takes out a cigarette.*) D'you want one?

She takes her own pack out of her coat pocket.

Ah! Not your brand . . . well, at least you're not one of those who smoke OP's . . .. Tons of them now saving money on our packs. The offices are full of them. Are you sure its OK for you to smoke? . . .. Well, I suppose you know best . . . it used to drive Mom crazy that you smoked. She figured it wasn't good for you – for your delicate health as she puts it . . .. As for me . . . well, I don't have an opinion about it, one way or another . . .. A woman smoking doesn't strike me as any uglier than a man smoking. It's like they always say: you got to change with the times. A woman isn't necessarily any more vulgar just because she smokes – you've got to be pretty narrow-minded to think that these days. Of course, when I was young it just wasn't done . . . only whores smoked on the street. Oh yeah, you saw a woman smoking on the street and you could go right up to her and ask her how much. Smoking and drinking . . . they just weren't things a woman did. Not that it kept them from doing it on the sly . . . there's a lot more of them were drinking than we'd ever thought . . .. As for me . . . well, I'll tell you a secret . . . a big secret . . . my mother . . . my own mother drank . . . oh, not a drop now and again . . . no, no, she drank, blind drunk, as they say . . . an alcoholic. Yeah . . . well, that's why I'm so careful. (*He shows her his almost empty glass.*) I keep pretty close tabs on myself, I hold back . . . because I know perfectly well that I could have a tendency that way . . .. Tonight, now, is a different story . . . I'm not so drunk that I don't know I've had more than my usual, but emotions ran pretty high today. It wasn't easy for me to do what I did. It wasn't easy, Chris. You'll understand that someday when you have kids of your own: there's some things, you might say, in life that are pretty tough going, there're things that can really knock the wind out of you. And kids . . . well, they're a little like parents . . . you might say that, finally, in the long run, they end up doing you just about as much harm as good. I'm talking in general now . . . about the kind of people I see . . . the guys at the office . . .. (*Pause.*) No, it didn't take me long, let me tell you, to figure out she was a drinker. She wasn't easy to get on with, my mother, she wasn't always *there* . . .. Just a kid, I can remember, she used to sing me songs and she'd be crying and crying over them, it was unbelievable. She used to scare me something fierce. She'd talk so loud, she'd make scenes, such a big commotion that my father'd say . . . he took off . . . he flew the coop . . . he just couldn't take it anymore – there was nothing he could do anyway . . .. She'd hide it everywhere: there wasn't a vinegar bottle in the house that had vinegar in it. In her perfume, in all her things – there was gin in every corner of the house. The minute she got her hands on a cent, we never had to wonder what she'd do with it – she'd take off looking for booze. Nobody knew. Not ever. My sister wasn't about to broadcast it. She took off, too. She managed to get herself married young and she never mentioned her again. Till after she was dead. Once my mother was dead, your aunt changed her tune. Then, it turned out, her mother was a saint who'd raised two kids all by herself, without any help from her terrible husband who'd walked out on her. I never said a thing. Never tried to correct her once . . . for a start because it seemed like it did her some good saying that, and then because it's none of my business. The only thing that's important to me is that nobody knows what she was like, that she had a drinking problem . . .. Mom doesn't know anything about it. And not a word about it from you either, she'd never forgive me, and for sure she'd say that that's where your weak stomach comes from. But it wasn't her stomach at all, it was her liver. And it killed her, too. You can't get away with that kind of drinking for long. Doesn't matter who you are. Not that it took her all that long either . . . I lived all alone with her from the time I was eighteen, when your sister – I mean, my sister, your aunt got married. And I stayed eleven years. Till she died. She had to be watched . . . so she wouldn't fall. Got to the point where she'd break an ankle or a wrist, just like that. But that was near the end . . .. No, it wasn't very pretty, near the end: she raved, she talked nonsense, I wonder if she even knew I was her son. Well, anyhow, I tried to forget it. I'll tell you the truth, I wish I could've forgotten her right then and there, like my sister did. She never laid eyes on her again, from the day she got married to the day she died. But I saw her. I saw her stoop lower than an animal, I saw her act like anything but a mother. And I always supplied her drink for her. For eleven years. All her drink. The stories and promises she'd make up to get me to get her her drink. I wasn't that much of a sucker. She never fooled me with her stories, her phony excuses and her endless bloody scenes. She'd just sit there thinking I fell for it. And I'd never say a thing: I just let it pass and I'd buy her her drink for just one reason: so she'd never go out like that. I didn't want anybody to know about it or to see her like that, with her face all wild, telling them her stupid stories so they'd feel sorry for her and give her a drink. I was ashamed of her. So I went out and bought her the drink myself. I never bought the gin at the same liquor store twice in the same month. I'd go all over town if I had to, or I'd buy it in another town or I'd manage to ask someone else to pick some up for me, as a favour – not often – only when I was really stuck . . .. Yeah, well, I just didn't want anyone to get suspicious, anyone at the liquor store or any of my friends. I'd have been so ashamed. I knew, and that was plenty. I kept her supplied with everything she needed – and that's saying some – and as for her, she stayed inside, in the house. That was our arrangement. She knew if she ever stepped one foot out of the house to go begging for a drink, she'd never get another drop from me. And I never budged an inch about that. I'd never been able to stand the shame if people knew. Never. And let me tell you, she stayed in the house. A wreck . . . in the end, she was a real human wreck. So finally I had to get the doctor in, and he told me it wouldn't be long if she kept drinking at that rate, wouldn't take much time at all before she was dead. And he was right! I tried to get her to stop. I tried even though I knew it wouldn't do any good. Anyhow, at least I told her what the doctor said. So she'd know what she was doing. But she . . . she was in so much pain, she threatened me, she said she'd go out on the street screaming that she was an alcoholic and that it was her own son who was pushing her to drink. See? Y'see . . .. I never guessed that she could've figured it out, that she'd know just exactly how to get me, that she knew that for me, the worst thing that could happen

– wasn't that she'd die, but that people would know. So I gave it to her. I gave as much as she wanted, and I'm not sorry. That's what she wanted, she made her own choice, all right, and that's all there was to it. (*Pause.*) It's funny you know, but there're times I think she hated me. Me, the only one who stayed with her, the only one who took care of her. A little while before she died she said to me, 'You thought I didn't know, hmm, you thought I didn't know that you were ashamed of your mother? Well, my little boy, you'll learn that when you spend your whole life being ashamed, all the time, with everybody, you learn to spot it in other people's faces. I've watched you being ashamed of me and ashamed for me since you were this tall . . . and it never taught you a thing, my poor ninny, it never taught you a bloody thing.' That's where she was wrong because it taught me to know when to draw the line with the bottle. I bloody well learned how to control myself: never go over your limit. I've never been as drunk as her, and I've never needed a drink as bad as her. I like to have a drink all right – even have a tendency that way – I don't deny it – but I know it and I can handle it. No one's ever gonna be ashamed of me – I promised myself I was never gonna be ashamed again . . . that's why no one knows. If Mom knew about it there'd be no end to it, looking out for signs, and thinking – there, that's it, I've become an alcoholic. No. She thinks my mother died of cancer of the liver and that's just perfect. She doesn't need to know any more about it, it wouldn't make a bit of difference in her life. (*Pause. He laughs to himself.*) What she doesn't know, though, is that actually it did make a bit of difference in her life . . .. A little while before she died, my mother started getting worried about my future. I don't know what came over her – she must have all of a sudden remembered she'd had kids. Anyhow, near the end she wouldn't stop asking me if I was gonna get married. She'd ask me how old I was, and then right after, every time, it never failed, she'd tell me how I had to get married, absolutely, 'to save myself from the

drink,' she'd say. As if marriage'd ever saved her from anything. Anyhow, she was wearing herself out and she was wearing me out so much with it that I finally said, yes, I was going to get married as soon as she got better. And then she started to laugh, and she said, well then, I'd be able to get married in two weeks 'cause she'd be dead and buried by then. And then, after that she started laughing at me, saying that I wasn't any better than her and that my story about getting married wasn't even true, that I'd just said it to get a little peace. Then she said she wasn't gonna die – just to piss me off, she said – she wasn't gonna die before she'd seen this woman. That's how my mother used to talk – she was always real blunt; it was the alcohol that did that to her. Oh, there was no end to the sweet talk when she wanted something, but once she got it, she'd tell you exactly what she thought, she had such a filthy mouth on her, she'd curse the whole world. Anyhow, I ended up having to bring somebody home to her just to get a little peace. So after we agreed that she'd say she had cancer of the liver, and not a word about the rest – so she wouldn't ruin my future – I decided to go ahead with it. In those days Mom was working as a secretary not far from my office. I'd just taken her out to a movie once, but that was it. So I asked her, as a favour, like, out of human kindness, I said. And she was willing. So I took her to see my mother, and it was my mother who planted the idea in her head that I'd be needing help after she was gone, I mean all sorts of crazy stories, her alcoholic bullshit: a *big* number. And Mom bought it all, the whole thing. When my mother died she even tried to find the funeral parlour and everything, but she never found it, 'cause I'd had her buried right away. But afterwards, later on, when I saw her again, after my mother was out of the picture, I started to appreciate her for herself. She was a very outgoing person, she'd never say anything out of place, she was a woman who had nothing to be ashamed of. So we got married – and you can see what a good deal it turned out to be: we get on and no arguments. Oh, we might've argued a little bit about you, back then, when you were first sick, but that's about it. If it hadn't been for you, and that sickness of yours when you were twelve, we'd've never raised our voices to each other. That's saying something, hmm?

CHRISTINE *gets up, carefully.*
ROLAND *assumes she's feeling sick.*

Again! You're not feeling any better? Christ, talk about a mess!

CHRISTINE *goes to the bathroom.*
ROLAND *stares at his glass and shakes his head.*

I think it's time to stop now. Before it starts playing tricks on me. Already, it's loosened my tongue without me even noticing. Yeah, that's enough now.

He empties his glass. Pause. He gets up, turns on the TV; snow, nothing else. He turns it off, goes to the window. CHRISTINE comes out of the bathroom, she looks at her father, wants to talk to him. He cuts her off.

OK? Feeling better now? What do you you say about going to bed and getting a little sleep, hmm? We've got a big day ahead tomorrow.

CHRISTINE *walks over and sits huddled on her bed.*

ROLAND *goes to the bathroom, returns, turns out the light and stretches out on the bed, fully dressed.*

I'll just stretch out a bit. Don't be embarrassed to wake me up if you need anything or if you're gonna be sick.

He turns out the lamp between their beds. We hear the rain. A single beam of light streams in through the window – a flashing neon if possible. A little time passes, and then in the dark we hear.

CHRISTINE: Your f-f-fa . . . your f- . . . f-ather?

Note: CHRISTINE is affected by a 'clonic', or specific, stutter. Therefore, keep strictly to those indicated, do not embellish. She stutters only on the letters 'F' and 'V'.

ROLAND (*surprised; still in the dark*):

My father? . . . I don't know . . . I really don't know. He must be dead by now . . . anyhow, as far as I'm concerned he's dead. He died when I was just a kid. Anyway, don't think about that anymore, it's not important, you're better off to forget it, I don't know why I even told you about it, it's stupid. Go to sleep. Close your eyes and try to sleep. I'll do the same. Good night, now.

Long pause. ROLAND is restless, tosses, unable to sleep. He lights a cigarette which provides the first glimmer of light in the dark room. The flashing light continues from outside the window. ROLAND smokes. From out of the near dark, we hear CHRISTINE's small voice.

CHRISTINE: Dad.

ROLAND: Wha-? You're not asleep? You scared me . . .. What's wrong? Are you sick again?

CHRISTINE: Am I too heav-v-vy f-f-fo-for you –

As soon as CHRISTINE starts to stutter, ROLAND abruptly turns on the bedside lamp. CHRISTINE immediately stops talking and instinctively, in a protective move, covers her face with her hands. It's an impulse that's stronger than her. He interrupts her.

ROLAND: Wait a minute, do you stutter like that because you're embarrassed? That's just what I said! That's what I always said. (*He puts out his cigarette.*) And there wasn't a single bloody specialist who'd believe me. It was too obvious for them, they wouldn't've been able to make any more money off me . . . when I think how we let ourselves get taken in by people like that who just take advantage of us, who'll get us to believe anything as long as it keeps us paying. It never did much good – did it – all that running back and forth to the specialists? All it did was make Mom crazy. You're still stuttering and my guess is you're gonna be stuttering for a long time to come. And to think how fast you started talking! You were making sentences when you were only two – you could say anything you wanted, not a hesitation, nothing. Your mother still has the pictures! It's school that did it to you, that ruined you – they must've embarrassed you, making you stand up and talk in front of everybody, so you started to stutter . . .. But you shouldn't worry about it, they say it has nothing at all to do with how smart you are. A person can be really intelligent and still stutter: they say there's no connection at all. If you could just get that through your head, I'm positive you'd stop in a second – and of course right away you'd seem smarter. I'm not saying at all that you're not already – don't get me wrong – I'm just talking about how it looks. And that's what people go by. You can't expect too much from people: they gotta go by what they see and what they hear. What can you expect, we don't always have a choice in the matter. For example, like, when I have to hire somebody for the store: now I have got to have something to go on, I've got to judge the applicant somehow. And what's gonna count most? His overall appearance. For sure if he squints or stutters, if he has any little fault like that it's gonna work against him. And that doesn't mean he's not a bright person, or even an intelligent person – but we have no way of knowing that and we don't have time to do a big investigation. No. When I'm hiring, it's the applicant's overall appearance I go by. (*He looks at her. Pause.*) I often ask myself what I'd do if a girl like you came into the store looking for work. I thought, well, if I wasn't biased, if you weren't my daughter, or anything. Let's say I didn't know you at all. Well, right off there's your speech defect. Because, see, you come across just fine – not a beauty or anything, but we're not running a modelling agency. No, you're pretty. A little on the skinny side but it's the style these days, what can you do. No, the only thing that would keep me from hiring you is the way you speak. Honestly, looking at it from the outside, when I take an objective view of it, it's absolutely clear that I could never hire you the way you are. I'm not saying I'd be happy about it, but the fact is you just can't plan on a job working

with the public. That, well that's an opening that's closed to you for just as long as you suffer from this handicap of yours. It's not for nothing that I pushed you so hard to get rid of it. It's the kind of thing that eats away at your future. And your future is important. Especially now. (*He smiles reassuringly.*) But don't you worry about that, kiddo, we'll manage to find you something – we'll just keep on looking until we do. I've got friends and contacts all over the place – even in a depression I could find you a job, just like that. You can thank your lucky stars you've got yourself a couple of responsible parents, Chris. I'm not asking for any thanks, that's not it, but just ask yourself how many young people fall into drugs because they're left on their own . . . Well, we're not quitters, we took on our responsibilities, we've done everything we could do for you, and we're gonna keep on doing it even if we don't have to anymore. We're not gonna turn our backs on you just cuz you're over eighteen. We're not that cruel. There's one thing you can always count on: you can be sure that your parents will always do their duty by you – and that's pretty rare – you'll find out soon enough. No, Mom and I always had one rule: if you have kids, look after them, make sure they've got what they need. You don't have kids just to leave them in misery. Better off to forget it.

He stands up, takes his glass from the table, fills it in the bathroom, returns.

Maybe it'll help me sleep, hmmm?

Pause. He looks at her, thoughtfully.

Yeah . . . I wonder what we're gonna do with you, Chris. It's no small thing – you've got your whole life ahead of you. You've got one helluva long haul to go yet. I used to think at least that we'd prepared you to manage a little on your own. See, Chris? You see? If you'd only been willing to finish college before getting married, you wouldn't be in such a bind right now. But no, you were in such a hurry, you were in such a hurry to throw yourself into the arms of that bum. Nineteen years old is just too young to get married. Way too young. OK maybe I waited a bit too long, but you Chris, well, you got married too young. Too young and – sorry to have to say it – to a real moron. OK, OK, we said we weren't gonna talk about it. I won't say another word about it. I just want to tell you one thing: don't think I'm gonna lay any blame here, but don't think that I'm gonna blame it all on him either. A couple is a couple: and if things are bad with a couple, it's pretty sure there's more than one person to blame. That's all I have to say on the subject. And you can rest assured, Chris, that I'm not the one who's gonna blame you. I just hope you've learned that you can't go throwing yourself into a marriage without thinking about it, without weighing the pros and the cons. I never said anything at the time because I wanted you to be free, because it was your choice, but that guy, let's just say I'd never've hired him at the store. If he'd ever come to me looking for a job, the answer'd've been: No thanks. And yet it's not that he looks so bad. But I'd still've said 'no'. Why? With a man, you've got to be a little more suspicious, you can't judge him the same way. With a man, I put a lot of trust in my overall impression. In a way, a woman's easier to hire. The standards are more specific, they're easier to pin down. But with a man, I don't know, it's a little more complicated, it's a little harder to know. See, in all honesty, I think I'd be more likely to make a mistake with a man, a male applicant. And also I hire a lot less of them. I'd be more inclined to be suspicious with a guy. With a woman I know right away what I'm dealing with, if she's a feather-brain or not; I know right away if I can get her to toe the line – if I'll have some kind of control over my staff. But before you even start, it's harder with a man. Harder to size up. First of all they're gonna recognise your authority a lot less, they tend to want to impress you, to show off what they can do right in front of you. Well, that kind of stuff puts me right off. I'd rather have someone who doesn't let on how well they know the job before they do it. I'd rather see a little humility. But real humility I mean.

Not lying and finagling just to get the job. I've got an incredible talent, a nose for people like that, the liars and the fakes. I swear to you there's not too many of them that ever got in at the store. And if there are any there now, it just shows you they weren't the kind of liars they thought they were. (*He knocks back the last of his drink.*) One last little one and then we'll get some sleep. I won't offer you one, hmmm, all right?

He goes to the bathroom to fill up his glass and returns. CHRISTINE *lights a cigarette nervously.*

Don't worry, hmmm, I know just where I am with it. I'll admit that I've had a little more than usual tonight; but you'll never see me blind drunk, don't worry.

He sits on the edge of his bed, facing her. The only indication of his advancing state might be a slight slowing down in the flow of his speech, emphasising certain words and concepts, and in his even greater candour.

Let's just say it makes me a little more open . . . and I'd rather be talking to you than to Mom. With you at least I know I'm not gonna hear any more about it later. You're not about to drag up what I've said and use it as evidence against me a month from now. No, with you it's almost like you never heard a word. Mom's a good woman, but when she finally manages to squeeze a little confession out of me, you know she's gonna make the most of it for one helluva long time to come. I don't know why she does it. you'd think she enjoyed it, you'd think she needed something to feel guilty about. Almost like she needed to keep feeding the guilt, to keep it going. Not me. Guilt, regrets – I don't know what they are. I got no use for them. I leave that to Mom. (*Pause. He laughs, softly.*) The last little while, I don't know what's wrong with her, she's always going on about sex. She got it into her head that I'm not getting enough of it, that she hadn't been a good wife to me, that I could just as easily have seen others, all sorts of bullshit like that. It must be her time of life that's got her talking that way . . .. Because there's certainly nothing I've said or done that could make her talk like that . . .. You know that, ah . . . after you . . . Mom couldn't have any more children. Anyhow the doctor said it was safer not to. Well, I could understand that, so from that moment on . . . we . . . ah . . . we never touched any of that again. I won't say I didn't think about it from time to time, but it's been a while since it crossed my mind. Well, I have to admit I'm over fifty . . . But I'll tell you it's more interesting up here. (*Taps his head.*) You know what I think? I think people have no imagination. We don't need sex all that much in life. I mean real sex, like, actually touching, and all. I guess I'm a pure spirit that way. I like to think about it a lot: for sure, I have lots of ideas, but I'd never actually touch that sort of thing. I don't understand a man paying a woman to sleep with her. Not me. I'd just like to watch her: I'd watch her walking around, doing whatever she does, and I'd keep her inside my head and, for the rest, well that's nobody's business but mine. I have a lot of respect for women. I'm certainly not the kind of man who'd ever touch them, abuse them, rape them. No, I'd be more the protector-type. I just don't like women being touched, it doesn't matter how, I just don't like it. And I gotta say that I don't like being touched either. No, I'd sooner look, dream about it, as they say – I'll never go further than that. Another kind of control, I guess (*Pause.*) It's funny, you know, there's this young girl at the store, real young, looks like a real baby – I used to like watching her fold the sweaters at her counter. She had a beautiful way of moving, a very special quality . . . I'd think about it a lot. Well, she got the idea that I was interested in her. And she started to act nice to me, always wanting to smile at me and all. Well that was the end of it. She ruined it for me. There was nothing to do about it. It just didn't work anymore, I couldn't think about her anymore. She'd spoiled my picture of her. It was like she'd lost . . . well, what you'd call her innocence. Like in that movie, *Bilitis*.

Well, I'd never seen anything that beautiful. I'd never've touched them either. Everything I like to look at was in that movie . . .. Those pictures turned over and over in my mind for one helluva long time, if you know what I mean. (*Pause. He laughs, embarrassed.*) It's a lucky thing your father isn't a skirt chaser, or a womaniser or anything or I'd've probably told you all about it tonight. No fear. I can even tell you about my sex life: no sweat, as they say, nothing there, to shock a girl of twenty. (*He chews on a cigarette.*) Oh, I'd love a cigarette now. I'm gonna tell you something, Chris. I'm gonna pay you a compliment. And it's not just because I've gone over my limit, oh no. I'm telling you because I think it'll give you a little encouragement, because you need to hear it after what's just happened to you.

In a very sensual tone: troubling and not at all fatherly.

I always have this picture of you in my head, the way you were when you were ten, eleven. You wouldn't believe how beautiful you were at that age. It's hard to believe but I'd never get tired of looking at you. Your hair was blonder, much fairer than it is now; hardly brown at all, and curly, a real little angel face. And you were just starting to develop . . . you were an early bloomer that way. You grew up all at once. Overnight you had a long, fine neck, and your lovely little head with your almost blonde hair, and your serious little look, and your little breasts that were just starting to bud . . . I'd never seen anything more beautiful. Yeah. One morning I said to Mom that you were already a beautiful young lady. I couldn't believe that you came from Mom. I couldn't believe that every day at home, in my own house, there was such a beauty for me to look at. You never realised it, but I used to look at you . . . that was way before I saw that film *Bilitis*, well, you were my first *Bilitis*. I was never so proud of you. In those days, I wouldn't have traded you for a boy for anything in the world. You could've asked me for anything, you'd've had it. Lucky for me you didn't suspect the slightest thing, eh, or you could've really cleaned up. Yeah, the year you were eleven – that's still what I think of when I think of you. My beautiful little eleven-year-old daughter. I never wanted time to pass, I never wanted anything to change. I would've just kept watching you like that, not saying anything, not touching, just seeing you like that was all I needed to be happy and I was. Mom was so happy that I was paying attention to you, that I was proud of you. No one could've been prouder. A little angel, a little angel, pure and untouched, that's just what you were, Chris. (*Pause. Bitter.*) That's just what you were before you fell sick and got as skinny as you did. Christ, you put one helluva scare into us. We came pretty close to thinking we were going to lose you. Skinny . . . talk about skinny . . . and stubborn and mean: never wanting to eat anything Mom made, sulking and hiding in your room all the time, and throwing up like just now . . . you never got that beautiful again, I never saw my girl again, my own little girl, my innocent little angel, my untouched Chris. You were just sick too long, it was such a long time before you were all right . . . but at least you got your health back I guess. Not real strong, but healthy. You'd lost your little girl look. That's for sure, hmmm . . . (*Pause.*) When you got out of the hospital, when I saw you again back at home – I can tell you now that you're OK – I couldn't look at you. I just couldn't, that's the truth. It was stronger than me. You looked like those pictures they used to show at the time, of Biafra, you know? And your eyes, your eyes seemed to take up your whole face . . . . I don't know, there's no way to say . . . they were eyes . . . like old people's eyes, no, uh . . . terrible eyes. I just couldn't look at you, I just couldn't bring myself to, it made me feel sick. I'd be remembering you at eleven and I'd see you there, at fifteen . . . I'm not kidding. You'd think they'd beaten you at the hospital. You look better now than you did then just to give you some idea. No, I'll never forget it. It's like they took away my dream, took away my little girl. And the specialists said

we didn't love you enough. If I didn't love you enough, I'd like to know what they think is enough, I'd like someone to come here and explain to me, right to my face, what's enough, just exactly what love is . . . *if* I loved you . . . I nearly went crazy with all that business with your eyes and your sickness, and the way you came back and all. For Mom, it was while you were sick that she almost went crazy. But for me, nobody knew about it, it was after, when you came back, when you weren't you anymore. Then . . . if anything could've made me fall into drink, that would've been it. It's like I couldn't recover from the disappointment. I just couldn't get over it. (*Pause.*) Not like the other one. You see how crazy the world is: there are only two things, only two real disappointments I ever had that could've really been dangerous to me, and both times I lost something. The first time was when Mom lost my boy. She was five months pregnant, and she had a miscarriage. We don't know why – a question of constitution, they said. I always said Mom shouldn't have been squeezing herself into those girdles. Of course she was bigger when she was pregnant but that's only normal, isn't it? Anyhow, I lost my little boy. He was called Christopher. I had him baptised and buried. It wasn't usually done but it was important to me. He was my son. The doctors said they couldn't be sure of the sex, but I could, it'd been five months that I'd been waiting for that child, and I knew he was a boy. The first, the oldest. It seems to me that I'd've been able to handle him, to talk to him, man to man, to make something of him, to build a future for him . . . but no. A year later you came. We named you Christine after him, and in spite of everything, we loved you. And there isn't a damned specialist anywhere who is gonna tell me any different. I remember you at eleven and I'm filled with tenderness all over again for the little girl you used to be. It's not something I was always telling you, for sure, I didn't go around announcing my love, but I'd look at you and you couldn't not feel that I loved you. But then I lost my beautiful girl too. I only ever dreamed of two things in my whole life: my little boy and my little eleven-year-old girl. Well, you see, both times I was so disappointed that I nearly fell to drinking. But I ended up understanding. I understood that it's better not to dream. Count your blessings and be thankful for what you've got.

Pause. He looks at her discouraged, tired.

And I have a big girl now, eh Chris? And, you see, I never let you down. You never even had to call me – I just came to get you. You can count on me, I'll never let you live with anybody who pushes you around, anybody who hurts you. You should learn how to defend yourself a little bit, not just give in. 'Cause, see, I might not always be there to take care of you, eh kiddo. But, we'll talk about that again tomorrow in the car. We gotta lie down and get some sleep now. You OK? Not sick?

She shakes her head slowly. He doesn't see her.

Anyhow, the little bit you ate shouldn't keep you throwing up all night, hmmm? That's all done with, lie down and get some sleep, hmm? Good night.

CHRISTINE *rocks herself, moaning, rocking herself harder and harder until she falls forward onto her knees. She then stands up and goes to the bathroom.*

The bathroom door is ajar. There's a large mirror on the outside of the door. CHRISTINE *looks at herself in the mirror, attentively, without moving. She stands before her reflection. Then she reaches for the doorknob, pulls it toward her, repeatedly slamming her face against the mirror. Harder and harder. Crying and almost mesmerised by the regular rhythm and her overwhelming despair.* ROLAND *wakes up with a start.*

What – What's – Chris! Are you sick?

He gets up and realises what CHRISTINE *is doing.*

Are you crazy? Are you out of your mind?!

He grabs her roughly and pulls her into the room.

What the hell's got into you to make you do such a stupid thing? What's wrong with you? You haven't had enough? 'S that it? He didn't beat you enough? You need more? You want more? Am I gonna have to lock you up to straighten you out? Am I gonna have to lock you away? Christ-All-Bloody-Mighty!

He slams the bathroom door. CHRISTINE *is standing at the door, in terror. Furious, he tries to get a hold of himself. He can hardly look at her.*

Listen to me Chris . . . I'm ready to believe you've been through some pretty rough times . . . and I'm ready to understand that you're tired and you're hurt and that you're maybe feeling bad about leaving your husband, even if he did treat you bad – I'm ready to be as understanding as you like . . . but you're gonna have to understand that I can't be watching you every second. You're not two years old anymore. And we're not, we're not real young anymore . . . you're gonna maybe have to take care of Mom more than you think. She's not all that well. She's not gonna be able to handle a girl who pulls stunts like this, that's for sure. And who spends the whole day throwing up. You can keep sucking away at us for just so long without giving anything back, Chris. You're just gonna have to grow up a little – otherwise I don't know what we're gonna do with you. We're not just gonna let you stay home, making a racket and dirtying the place up . . . Mom just can't handle it anymore. And I'm not sure I can take it either. OK? Do we understand each other now? You're gonna have to be reasonable, and show a little consideration cause we're just too old for this. Now be a good girl, and try to understand.

CHRISTINE *starts slamming her head again, backwards this time, against the wall or door. She closes her eyes and slams, slams, as if trying to make her head and the pain explode. Her father rushes at her, grabbing her roughly to pull her away from the wall. Then, in a rush, he gets his suitcase, his coat from the closet and grabs her by the arm.*

Let's go. Come on, we're going.

She pulls her arm away and backs off.

CHRISTINE: No!

ROLAND: I said: we're going!

CHRISTINE *is in terror. She backs away again toward the bathroom. She shakes her head rhythmically and repeats with each shake:*

CHRISTINE: No . . . no . . . no . . .

ROLAND (*beside himself, screaming*): I'm not taking you to the nut house, I'm taking you home. Do you understand? *HOME!*

CHRISTINE (*wild with terror, she screams too, now*): N-O-O-O!

ROLAND: Jesus Bloody Christ! That's enough!

He drops his bag and his coat, and strides over to her, utterly determined. CHRISTINE *backs into the bathroom and closes the door. He rushes for the doorknob and shakes the door violently.*

Out here! Right now. Out! Or I'll break it down!

He shakes the doorknob and in one swift move opens the door. Immediately we hear the sound of a bottle being broken against the sink. ROLAND *freezes, stunned. He backs into the room!*

Don't touch that . . . don't touch that . . . don't touch.

CHRISTINE *comes out of the bathroom weeping, the broken gin bottle in her hands. She holds it as a weapon but we can't tell whether it's meant to be used offensively or against herself. She keeps her father at a distance. She murmurs through her tears, all the while shaking her head, no, as if overcome by the horror.*

CHRISTINE: I don't want to kill myself . . . .
I don't want to kill myself . . . .
I don't want to kill myself . . . .

As if she were trying to find a way out of a dilemma by repeating these words. ROLAND, *seeing her motionless, approaches her very cautiously. He holds out his hand to her and says softly, as if to a madwoman . . . . He is very frightened.*

ROLAND: Give, Chris . . . give it to Daddy . . . give it to Daddy . . . be a good girl.

Abruptly, she looks at him and slashes his arm with the bottle, missing his hand. She throws herself at him and cuts his eyes with a terrible force. They fall between the two beds, she on top of him. She lashes out, relentlessly, drawing back her arm after each blow, as if gathering strength from the building momentum. With each blow, from the first to the last she shouts:

CHRISTINE: You want to kill me . . . you want to kill me . . . you want to kill me . . . .

At the end of her strength, she propels herself away from him, still crying, her hands full of blood.

Lights fade down and out.

Night

I wrote *L'Homme gris* (*Night*) under the influence of some sort of visual obsession: without knowing where this man was going or what he really wanted, I kept seeing him entering the motel, driven by the rain and his bad mood, holding his two boxes of barbecued chicken at arm's length and looking back towards the door opened to the storm (to his daughter) and then calling her without saying her whole name.

I knew where he was coming from, I knew of course that he had gone to retrieve this so 'troublesome' daughter in order to 'save' her and that this terrible night would lead to the climax of his undertaking: to carry out the moral destruction of his daughter, carry out this verbal 'execution' of her, done without a shred of awareness on his part.

Unconsciousness has always deeply disturbed me. Unconsciousness seems to me like a perfect knife that commits so many murders without ever staining its blade. No blood, no odour: oh! if only Lady Macbeth had known . . .

How is a play born, from what maze of conscious desires, of deep, violent urges, of incomplete reasonings and flashes of intuition? I never know. Writing *L'Homme gris* required years of preparation on my part: for a long time I have tried to understand why a woman is beaten by her mate, where does it originate? The causes are many, profound and complex. But always, they take root in the woman's self-respect or rather, some kind of lack of self-respect. And then, little by little, I became aware of another order of causes, I understood the ravages made possible by love, not only the love that goes unheeded, but the refusal, the rejection of the other's love, of its very nature. To her father, Christine was anything but satisfying: a weight, a duty, a sacrifice, a mistake from the start, a basic mistake.

L'Homme gris is not the story of Roland Fréchette, it is not a one-man show. It is the story of a childhood (in fact, of two childhoods), a terrible childhood because it is perfect and perfectly destroyed by perfection itself. All the standards for raising a child were respected. And yet . . .

For me the theatrical challenge was to make the whole drama clear without having Christine reproach her father, since she lacks the self-confidence required for reproach. Her presence, the way she listens attentively (and sometimes painfully) to her father's words, while the audience identifies with her feelings, her presence, were meant to bring out Roland's unconscious cruelty and make it unbearable for the audience.

Christine does not speak for a very simple reason: she knows her father, she knows how she exasperates him, and she does not want to displease him. She knows full well that the best way of winning some indulgence from her father is by being silent. Christine must once have attempted to speak (stuttering the 'p's' of Papa, for sure . . .) but the only way out for her now is silence. For a long time, her father has not been *listening* to her. For a long time, he has viewed her as a reflection of his personal success (or failure) and not as an independent person with her own reactions and private feelings. This is partly why the only thing that comes out of her mouth is food (while her father drinks non-stop, literally filling himself up). Her vomiting 'catches' Roland's eye; that is the sort of speech that he understands and respects (at least it shuts him up). And it's not manipulation on Christine's part, it's her emergency exit. Tracked down, pursued, horrified, she doesn't know how to scream, she only knows how to reject the food that comes from her father, in a gesture of self-defence that actually only frees her from this unbearable conversation.

Had Christine succeeded sometime in her life in hating her father this story would never have been written.

The absolute love, without judgement, without restriction, that she has always felt for her father (without ever any 'bargaining') is the very instrument of her destruction. One has only to listen to Christine speaking to her father in the darkness once she has been reassured and elated by the implicit complicity of sharing the secret of his alcoholic mother. This moment of friendship, of definite pleasure, of Roland's acceptance of Christine (since he has honoured her with a secret) is so important to her that she allows herself to ask him what his own father did to him (unable as she is even to imagine that a father might not have any influence on his child).

Christine's love, her vital need (the term is excruciatingly apt) to be recognised, her need of love as a sort of proof of her own importance, places her in a suicidal position. If Christine were able to break away from this man, to no longer wish that he love her, or only appreciate or see her, she would be saved, she would send him packing. But there it is: to send him packing, she would have to find in herself some kind of strength and confidence and she is barely formed, barely developed as a personality since she has always lacked the essentials. She is known by her father only as an imperfection, a miss, a failure of some sort. And if ever she gets angry, she has absorbed her father's message so well that she takes it out on herself.

Seen from this angle, the crisis brought on by the father's desire is perhaps easier to understand. Is it necessary to point out that Roland Fréchette is an incestuous father, utterly incestuous, even if he does not physically touch his daughter? The voyeur's stare he has given her is a stare without innocence. Still torn between her desire to have her father 'look' at her (an insane desire to be 'recognised') and her violent refusal of this sexual behaviour (which she was very clearly decoding, contrary to what her father was thinking), how could Christine escape? What choice was there between two deaths? How to scream without driving him away? How can she change her father's eyes staring at her, beseech them not to consume her (as a vulgar sexual object) but to help her by 'seeing' her as herself, by loving her?

I believe that Christine's anorexia is an urgent appeal, a desire to control something in her life where everything eludes her. If she cannot control her father's stare, at least she will control the coveted object so desired, so outrageously abused by this look. In the anorexia is the mad hope of being grasped for what she is; it is a vibrant call for help, a terrible void that is screaming for assistance. By calling on what little strength she has in order to remain whole, to persist, to take on the physical appearance of the void she feels within herself, Christine ends up by carrying in her body the changed look that she sought from her father.

If Roland is fooled by his admission of long-standing desire and of his way of consuming it, of having sex with her, by this thinly disguised 'innocent' admission, barely veiled by the mist of paternal love, then he is the only one who is.

Christine's final attack stems from what she feels is unbearable in this confession. She cannot accept learning about it. And it's not because her life seems so important to her. It's mostly because what little shred of dignity she still clings to can only survive if her father's desire remains unspoken. She would have rather died than admit to herself what is inadmissible: that her father desired her sexually and that she had never succeeded in being anything else in his eyes. Even if her anorexia proves that she was aware of his desire, the final attack proves that she never consciously recognised or accepted it. Christine was savagely refusing to give a 'name' to incest, to reveal it to herself. It's no accident that she first attacks the eyes, that his eyes are what she seeks to destroy.

Christine's escape into anorexia was her way of screaming in silence, of holding back the obscene stare while hoping to change it. But Roland doesn't hear Christine. Dazzled by his own deception, dazzled by the alcohol that helps him to relax his own self-control, he breaks out and evokes the only people who were important in his life: his mother and his daughter. He still wants to have power over Christine. This man who is terrified of women can think only in terms of dominance and authority where one person wins. Crushing the other person is the only way he knows of reassuring himself and winning the game. Roland has remained forever a desperate, abandoned child, madly attempting to fill parental expectations (in this instance, society's) with a normality that is proof of his good intentions in the hope, for him too, of being loved – even if he ignores it himself. But he is better equipped than Christine to whom he has bequeathed only his suffering.

All suffering that is silenced, repudiated or suppressed is liable to reappear in our human relationships to destroy and crush tenuous emotional ventures. Once the pain has been brought to light, maybe it doesn't hurt less, but the knife at least has lost some of its edge and the weapon becomes less dangerous. Crying is not a comfort in itself, but it might be the most human part of what we are.

Marie Laberge

I have written eighteen plays.

In chronological order of writing, they are the five short pieces collected under the title *Profession: je l'aime* which include, in addition to the title play, *On a ben failli s'comprendre*, *T'sé veux dire*, *La fille fuckeuse de gars* and *Eva et Évelyne* (VLB Editeur, 1986). These plays all deal with the complex and, more often than not, impossible nature of male-female relationships.

Ils étaient venus pour . . . (VLB Editeur, 1981) is a drama of epic style relating the twenty-five years of existence of a turn-of-the-century country village that has been abandoned for lack of political will when the mill, around which the entire village revolved, closed down.

Avec l'hiver qui s'en vient is a play revolving around the lack of communication within a couple. A 65-year-old woman, after a rather difficult life, finds herself obliged to take care of her recently retired husband. He is depressed and declining, no longer finding any taste for life now that he is at home. A drama that leads to an inevitable clash (VLB Editeur, 1982).

Le Bourreau is, in my opinion, a failed play about the death penalty. A sort of philosophical allegory that doesn't have the quality of its pretensions.

Jocelyne Trudelle trouvée morte dans ses larmes (VLB Editeur, 1983) is one of my favourite plays. A musical drama (one of the characters expresses herself only through song) about suicide at twenty. A cruel play that does not beat about the bush, but one that is essential to me.

I wrote *C'était avant la guerre à l'Anse à Gilles* (*Before the War, Down at l'Anse à Gilles*, translated by Allan Brown) immediately after *Jocelyne Trudelle* to comfort myself after the horrible violence of the latter. It is a chronicle of the way of life in the Québec countryside in 1936 during the Depression. Loving, warm, appealing characters and . . . drama and violence none the less (VLB Editeur 1981).

Le Banc is a kind of kaleidoscopic view of urban life and people who meet and cross paths in a city park, almost without seeing each other. All sorts of people, miseries, ages and concerns. A kind of character gallery tinged, this time, with some humour.

Deux tangos pour toute une vie (VLB Editeur, 1985) is another play focusing on a couple, but this time in their thirties. About the couple and about passion. Impossible and unattainable passion. Passion that is all-consuming and (miraculously) challenging everything . . . even the couple itself.

L'Homme gris (*Night*, translated by Rina Fraticelli; VLB Editeur, 1986 and *Revue Avant-Scène théâtre* no. 785 for the European French version) that you have just read. Also translated into Dutch, German and Italian.

Au bord de la nuit is a play that concerns itself with madness, a 30-year-old woman's severe identity crisis. Between fascination and the terrible fear that madness incites.

Le Night Cap Bar (VLB Editeur, 1987) is a play that dramatises, under cover of a 'Whodunnit', alcoholism, addiction and the kind of ambition that money triggers. Also some cruelty, once everything human has been drunk.

Oublier (*Take Care*; VLB Editeur, 1987) involves four sisters who meet at the bedside of their mother who is dying of Alzheimer's disease. They have in common a fierce love (which for some has changed to hatred) for their mother, and also some family accounts to settle. (English translation by Rina Fraticelli and European French version also available.)

Aurélie, ma soeur (upcoming publication, VLB Editeur 1988). A play about Aurélie who has raised Charlotte, her sister's daughter, as her own child since shortly after the child's birth. A tender, tender play, about the love that sometimes enables us to overcome all disasters.

Le Faucon, my very latest play on which ink has not yet dried! A confrontation between a young man of seventeen suspected of having killed his stepfather, and his therapist, a former nun of fifty-one, and his real father, who has returned after a total twelve-year absence.

Finally, while writing this summary, I realise that my themes are oh! so ultra light (death, love, madness, solitude . . .) and indeed, of the sort 'never seen before' . . . I suppose they all find their *raison d'être* in their dramatic treatment.

Marie Laberge

Rina Fraticelli

Rina Fraticelli is presently Executive Producer of Studio D, the Woman's Studio of the National Film Board of Canada. From 1982-86 she was Artistic Director of Playwrights' Workshop Montreal, where she developed *Transmissions*, a programme which workshopped Canadian and Québecois plays in translation. Ms Fraticelli has worked as dramaturg at a number of Canadian theatres, including Factory Theatre, Alberta Theatre Projects, Théâtre Expérimentale des Femmes, Nightwood Theatre, the National Arts Centre and the Banff School of Fine Arts Playwrights' Colony. Ms Fraticelli is the author of '1982 Study on the Status of Women in Canadian Theatre'. This is her first translation.

EFFIE'S BURNING

Valerie Windsor

Effie's Burning was first produced by the Library Theatre Company, Manchester, as part of its Lunchtime Season in April 1987, with the following cast:

EFFIE PALMER   Paula Tilbrook
DR KOVACS   Brigit Forsyth

Directed by Susan Sutton Mayo
Designed by Phil Daniels
Lighting designed by Tim Wratten

Effie's Burning was scheduled to open at the Bush Theatre, London, in 1987, but as a result of fire there, and with the co-operation of the Bush, the play was given three lunchtime performances and two evening performances at the National Theatre. It then had a four-week run at Offstage Downstairs, London.

A hospital room. There is one bed, a bedside locker and a chair. Beyond the bed is an empty area.

The bed is empty and the covers thrown back as if someone had just vacated it to go to the lavatory, which is indeed the case.

After a moment EFFIE *wanders in. She is limping slightly: her feet hurt.* EFFIE *is a woman in her sixties. She has been badly burned. Her face, her hands and arms etc., are affected. Despite her age and her injuries she has an untouched, childlike quality.*

EFFIE: Just been to toilet, Alice. (*There is, of course, no response. Slightly warily as if she suspects Alice may be teasing her:*) Alice? (*A pause. Nervously:*) Alice? (*She looks round suspiciously.*) Where'm she gone? (*She considers the situation, then a comforting solution occurs to her.*) Alice gone to toilet as well. (*She pats the bed proprietorially. This is the routine she uses to comfort herself.*) This is my bed . . . (*And then indicating beds which aren't there:*) That's Alice's bed. That's Dot's bed. (*She may repeat this while she takes off her dressing-gown just to make sure.*)

During this, DR RUTH KOVACS *enters. She comes into the empty area. In one hand she holds a sheaf of disorganised notes which she is trying to read. The other hand is trying to pin up a strand of hair that keeps falling down. She has a thrown together, slightly harassed look. She drops several pieces of paper, bends to pick them up and, on rising, begins to speak to the audience.*

DR KOVACS: Sorry. (*She sorts through the notes. A sudden thought:*) What do you call magistrates? Are they 'Your worships'? (*Slightly apologetically:*) I've never done anything like this before. I assume they just ask questions. Do they? Like in court. Well, obviously. It *is* a court. But do they expect . . . (*Still trying to get the notes in some sort of order.*) Oh God . . . this is all out of order now . . . hang on. Hang on. (*A statement of her intention:*) I will do this.

(*Assuming some authority:*) Your worships, I have been treating Miss Effie Palmer for the last three weeks . . .

At the sound of her name, EFFIE *looks up and answers obediently but dully as if answering a register.*

EFFIE: Yes, Miss.

DR KOVACS (*turning to speak to her about this 'Yes Miss' business*): Effie!

EFFIE: Yes, Miss.

DR KOVACS: Yes Miss, yes Miss, yes Miss. Try No Miss for a change.

EFFIE: No, Miss.

DR KOVACS: 'No, Miss', you won't try saying 'No, Miss' for a change, or . . .?

EFFIE (*dully*): I don't know, Miss.

DR KOVACS *looks at her for a moment, worried by her mood, then returns to what she was doing.*

DR KOVACS (*to the audience, using the notes*): The patient, Effie Palmer . . .

EFFIE (*dully, to herself*): Yes, Miss.

DR KOVACS: . . . was committed to Crampton Court mental hospital apparently under Section 2 of the 1913 Mental Deficiency Act in . . . as far as I can make out from various conversations with her . . . 1936. The original records were moved during the war and subsequently lost. The patient is now sixty-four, but has an estimated mental age of ten.

EFFIE (*looking up, suddenly anxious*): Miss?

DR KOVACS: What?

EFFIE: Where's Alice gone?

DR KOVACS: Oh, Effie . . .

EFFIE (*panic rising because of a bad memory she can't quite get hold of*): This is my bed . . . this one . . . that's Alice's bed. That's Dot's bed.

DR KOVACS: At Crampton Court, Effie. Not here.

EFFIE: Somerville Ward. That's us, Miss. Somerville.

DR KOVACS: Yes, I know . . .

EFFIE: It's a nice name, Miss. En it? Like summer. Somerville. And we'm got yellow curtains and yellow mats, Miss, with stripes. By our beds. And we got a big day-room and my chair is the blue one by the tele. (*She looks round. Sudden and growing panic:*) Where is this? I don't know where I am? Where's Alice gone . . .?

DR KOVACS (*patiently*): You know about Alice . . .

EFFIE: I don't like this room. I don't like the way the walls are. Miss, my arms hurt. I hurt . . .

DR KOVACS: In the beginning she wouldn't speak to me. 'There's some batty old bird in Room 7,' said Mr Jessop Brown.
    No he didn't. He didn't say that. Be fair. But I knew what he meant.
    'See if you can get any sense out of her, Dr Kovacs,' he said. 'Doctor.' With that slight sneer that means he expects nothing from me. Nothing. Except possibly the worst. Which, of course, is what he looks forward to. Vindication. 'There you are, you see, what did I always say?'
    'More your territory, I'd have thought,' he said. As if one of us were trespassing. Here. On his wards.
    'Effie Palmer,' he said. 'Some sort of pyromaniac, apparently. Set her bed on fire. Burnt the house down.'

DR KOVACS *goes into* EFFIE's *room.*

Good morning. I'm Dr Kovacs.

But the moment DR KOVACS *entered,* EFFIE *rolled over and pulled the single sheet up over her head.*

(*Awkwardly, a little louder:*) Good morning. (*No response.*) Are you asleep? (*No response.*) I'd like to have a look at your arms, please, Miss Palmer.

There is still no movement or response. She looks at the charts at the bottom of the bed partly in order to waste time while she thinks what to do next.

I'll ask a nurse to come.

EFFIE (*muffled noise from under the cover*): Don't want a bloody nurse.

DR KOVACS: What? (*She tries again.*) Miss Palmer, I'm a doctor. I'm here to look at your burns.

No response.

(*To the audience:*) Now what? Now what do you do? I used to think a white coat equalled authority. It doesn't.

She considers the situation.

What would Mr Jessop Brown do? Mr Jessop Brown would say . . . in the voice he uses for old ladies and difficult children . . . 'Now what's all this silly nonsense about, eh?' And pull off the sheet as swiftly and skilfully as he slices skin sections ready for grafting.

(*To* EFFIE, *attempting friendly authority:*) What's all this nonsense about, eh? (*She reaches out to pull away the sheet, but her hand stops.*)

(*To the audience:*) Why should I? If she doesn't want me to look at her burns . . .
    No, that's stupid. That's just an excuse. Freedom of the individual etc. Playing about with moral arguments to hide the fact that when *I* say things like that nobody takes a blind bit of notice.
    Mr Jessop Brown would say: 'Well, then, get the ward sister, get a nurse.'

The need to say something overcomes her. She comes out of the room and into the space. EFFIE, *surprised at having been left, peers suspiciously over the top of the sheet.*

(*To the audience:*) I'll tell you something shameful now. The reason I became a doctor.
    The reason I became a doctor was because . . . (*Having started off confidently she crumbles:*) . . . you see, I don't know really. I look back and try to think where the moments of choice were . . . where I deliberately made a choice between this path and that. And I can't see any. Like a conveyor belt. Once on . . . (*Using her mother's Middle European accent:*) 'Oh Ruthie, Ruthie,' my mother said. 'A doctor! A doctor in the family. If your Grandmother Kovacs had only lived to see this.'

What I really wanted to do . . . was something delicate, something skilful like picture restoring . . . because I do, I actually do quite like restoring things. But *things* not people. Comprehensible, inanimate things. Beautiful things. Smooth, ordered surfaces. Cool, pale colours.

'Well, Dr Kovacs,' he said, 'have we examined our troublesome patient in number 7?'

'No, sir. Not exactly. Not yet. I'm . . . I'm just on my way.'

She goes back towards the room.

There was a policewoman coming out. (*As if to a policewoman:*) Good morning.

She enters. EFFIE *is in a defensive position against the pillows. There is a set expression on her face.*

Good morning. I'm Dr Kovacs. I came in to see you earlier, but . . . (*She trails off.*) I came . . . I just wanted to have a quick look at your arms, that's all.

EFFIE *sticks out her arms.*

This one first. (*She starts undoing the dressing.*) How did it happen?

No response. Then EFFIE *winces and instinctively tries to withdraw her arm.*

Sorry. There's a slight infection in here. Where does it hurt most? There? Under the arm?

EFFIE: Yes, Miss.

DR KOVACS: You know to keep the arms up as much as possible, don't you. In the air. Like that. And move them. So the skin here (*Under the armpit.*) keeps flexible.

EFFIE: Yes, Miss.

DR KOVACS: I'm not a miss. I'm a doctor.

EFFIE: Yes, Miss.

Pause.

Where's Alice gone?

DR KOVACS: Who?

EFFIE: Alice.

DR KOVACS: Who's Alice?

EFFIE: This is my bed. That's Alice's

bed. That's . . .

DR KOVACS: Which is Alice's bed?

EFFIE: That one.

DR KOVACS: There isn't a bed.

EFFIE: Yes, there is. At Crampton Court there is. Somerville Ward.

DR KOVACS: What about your face? Any trouble with the eyelids?

EFFIE: You tell her, Miss?

DR KOVACS: Tell who?

EFFIE: They come asking me questions. I don't know what I got to say.

DR KOVACS: Oh, you mean the policewoman?

EFFIE: Tell her I didn't have no matches.

DR KOVACS: What about opening your eyes in the morning?

EFFIE: Knock knock.

DR KOVACS: Pardon?

EFFIE: It's a joke I know, Miss.

DR KOVACS: That's clever. I never know any jokes. I don't know why.

EFFIE: I know one. Knock, knock. You got to say: 'Come in'.

DR KOVACS: Come in. (*A thought:*) No, don't I have to say 'Who's there?'

EFFIE: Noah.

DR KOVACS: Pardon?

EFFIE: Noah, you can't come in.

They stare at each other blankly for a moment. It has not turned out quite as either of them expected and neither of them can quite work out what went wrong.

I read that in a comic once.

DR KOVACS (*lying*): It's very good. (*After a pause:*) No, I think I should have said . . . I don't think . . . I know, shall we start again?

EFFIE: No.

DR KOVACS (*snubbed*): All right.

EFFIE: You going now?

DR KOVACS: In a minute.

EFFIE: Right.

DR KOVACS: Yes.

A pause.

EFFIE: You coming back?

DR KOVACS: I expect so, yes. It depends.

EFFIE: I don't like them doctors.

DR KOVACS: I'm a doctor.

EFFIE *looks at her suspiciously.*

EFFIE: I thought you was something different.

DR KOVACS: No.

EFFIE: I thought you was.

DR KOVACS: Like what?

EFFIE: Don't ask no silly questions, my mum said, you won't get told no lies.

DR KOVACS: It wasn't a silly question. Was it?

EFFIE: I don't know who you are, do I? There's all sorts. They come in here. I can't remember them all. Social workers. Community workers. Psych . . . psych . . .

DR KOVACS: Psychiatrists.

EFFIE: Them as well. (*A pause.*) You was going.

DR KOVACS: Yes.
    Keep your arms up. It'll stop any swelling.

EFFIE: Tell 'em I never had no matches.

DR KOVACS: I'll come and see you tomorrow, shall I?

There is no response, but when DR KOVACS *has left the room,* EFFIE *holds her arms up for a short while until they get tired.* DR KOVACS *has moved into the space.*

'Yes, all right,' I said. 'I'll do it.'
    'Very keen all of a sudden,' said Mr Jessop Brown. 'However . . . however . . . since Dr Kovacs is obviously on the same wavelength ha ha as our problematic patient in Room 7, let us leave her to it.'
    And we . . . his little team . . . his white-coated phalanx of registrars and housemen . . . we all laugh. On cue. Ha ha. And we trot along the corridors behind him, our white coats flapping, all jostling to get his ear, to catch his attention. And they're all thinking: 'Thank God for Ruth Kovacs. Thank God it's her he's got it in for, and not me.' I can hear them thinking it. And the relief makes their laughter that little bit wilder. My hair is escaping. There's a ladder in my tights. There's a burning at the back of my eyes. No, please, please, whatever else please don't let me cry.
    Cry? Good lord, no. Ha ha, as I scramble along in the rear, trying to keep up. Ha ha, in case anyone should think I haven't got a sense of humour, in case anyone should say; 'Oh come on, Ruth, can't you take a joke?'
    Joke? *Joke?*
    The thing I liked about Effie . . . one of the things I liked about Effie . . . was that she didn't understand about jokes either.

She moves towards the room. As she enters.

EFFIE: Knock knock.

DR KOVACS (*trying to get it right this time*): Who's there?

EFFIE: You are. And I didn't hear no knocking.

DR KOVACS: No, I'm sorry. In hospital we . . .

EFFIE (*suddenly*): I never did it, Miss.

DR KOVACS: Never did what?

EFFIE: That place they took us to. The Laurels. They said I done it on purpose. Stole the matches and set my bed on fire.

DR KOVACS: And did you?

EFFIE: I didn't have no matches. I told you.

DR KOVACS: So how did it start?

EFFIE *tightens her mouth. No response.*

It was a very bad fire. Not just the bed.

EFFIE: Didn't say it was just the bed. Said it started in the bed.

DR KOVACS: How?

EFFIE *shuts her mouth tight.*

It's OK. It doesn't matter to me. I just . . .

EFFIE: So what you come for then?

DR KOVACS: I've come to look at your arms.

EFFIE: It's my face hurts now.

DR KOVACS: Let's undo the dressing, shall we?

She starts undoing the dressing on EFFIE's *head.*

EFFIE: You can if you want. You one of them social workers?

DR KOVACS: No, I'm a doctor.

EFFIE: You come to spy on me?

DR KOVACS: No, of course not.

EFFIE: Funny name, Kovacs.

DR KOVACS: It's Czech. Well, German. Well, no, Czech. My family came . . . it's difficult to say precisely. We say from Czechoslovakia. The Sudetenland. Sometimes it was one thing, sometimes another. Depending. On who was in power. Not us, that's for certain. Shoved here. Pushed there. We landed up stateless refugees. Until we crept through the back door into this country. 'Don't complain, don't complain,' my mother used to say. 'Answer nicely. Don't rock the boat, we've got our freedom, that's enough.'

EFFIE *snorts. Then:*

EFFIE: You German, then?

DR KOVACS: I'm not anything really. British now.

EFFIE: You're a doctor.

DR KOVACS: Yes.

EFFIE: I don't like that one what came in a suit.

DR KOVACS: Mr Jessop Brown?

EFFIE: I don't like him.

DR KOVACS: No, nor do . . . (*Realises this is indiscreet.*) I think we can leave the dressing off now. Careful not to touch it.

EFFIE: I seen men like him before. Bossy men. Men who get everybody rushing round like chickens when the fox gets in the barn. My dad was a bossy man. (*Suddenly getting upset. In a rush, her comfort routine:*) This is

my bed, that's Alice's bed, that's Dot's bed. I don't like it. I don't like it here. Them walls. Too close in. I want to go home.

DR KOVACS: Where is home?

EFFIE: Where I live. The blue chair close to the tele. That's mine.

DR KOVACS: Somerville Ward?

EFFIE: It's better than Anderson, Miss. I don't like them on Anderson. Mavis. She'm spiteful. She hits people if she'm in a bad mood. She pulled my hair once. (*Suddenly, alarmed:*) Where's Alice?

DR KOVACS (*confused*): What?

EFFIE: Alice is my friend.

DR KOVACS: I'll try and find out for you, shall I? Alice who?

EFFIE: Alice . . . (*Thinks. Irritably.*) She come when I come. Same day I think it was. Round about. She had long hair in a plait and they cut it off. And they never give her back her ribbon.

DR KOVACS: This was when you came to Somerville Ward?

EFFIE: Crampton Court.

DR KOVACS: That's what I mean.

EFFIE: Wasn't on Somerville straight away. It's the special ward for the very good ones. (*With pride.*) I been there years.

DR KOVACS: How long?

EFFIE: Years.

DR KOVACS: How many years?

EFFIE: Oh . . . years and years and years . . .

DR KOVACS: Ten?

EFFIE: Somerville. Crampton Court Hospital, Draycott. That's my address, Miss. England. The World.

DR KOVACS: You got letters?

EFFIE: Letters?

DR KOVACS: Can you remember your address before that, Effie?

EFFIE: No, I never got no letters, Miss. What do you mean?

DR KOVACS: Before you went to Crampton Court. Where did you live? Didn't your mother write to you?

EFFIE (*thinking hard*): My mother . . . (*A great pain washes over her and slowly, out of it, a memory emerges.*) On the farm.

DR KOVACS (*probing hard*): You lived on a farm?

EFFIE (*the memory is painful*): . . . the farm . . .

DR KOVACS: When you were a little girl?

A pause. EFFIE struggles to think. Then a broad smile crosses her face.

EFFIE: Do you know what my real name is, Miss?

DR KOVACS: Effie isn't your real name?

EFFIE: No, Miss.

DR KOVACS: So what is?

EFFIE: Gloria.

DR KOVACS: Gloria!

EFFIE: Out of this film my mum saw. Some film star. My dad said: 'What do you want to waste a name like that on her for?'

I never told no one that, Miss.

He said: 'She'm daft in the head. You don't want to waste no posh name on her.'

DR KOVACS: Gloria Swanson.

EFFIE: 'Don't want to waste no posh name on that effing brat.' (*A pause. She smiles.*) So he called me Effie.

A pause.

DR KOVACS (*shocked*): You made that up.

EFFIE: I didn't.

DR KOVACS: Effie short for effing?

EFFIE: Yes, Miss.

A pause.

DR KOVACS: I don't believe it. You're telling stories.

EFFIE: Short for effing brat.

DR KOVACS: Either you made that up or you've got it all wrong.

EFFIE (*face completely closed*): Yes, Miss.

DR KOVACS (*feeling blustery*): You must've done.

EFFIE: Yes, Miss.

DR KOVACS (*which flares into irritation*): Will you stop saying 'yes, Miss'.

Pause. EFFIE stares at her expressionlessly.

EFFIE: Yes, Miss.

This is pointless. DR KOVACS gets up.

DR KOVACS: I'll come and see you tomorrow. (*Suddenly forestalling EFFIE:*) And don't say it. All right? Don't say it.

She comes out of EFFIE's room looking flustered and upset.

I didn't believe a word of it. Not a word.

'Mind not entirely on your work, Dr Kovacs?'

Not really, no, Mr Jessop Brown.

No, I didn't say that. Of course I didn't. 'Sorry,' I said. 'I'm awfully sorry.'

I don't know why that stupid story upset me so much.

'Dr Kovacs is not entirely with us this morning, it seems.'

Poor old Ruth, getting it in the neck again. Ha ha. Listen to them snigger sycophantically. And in my head I say, 'Stuff you, Mr Jessop Brown'. But all the time my mouth's laughing, and my feet scurry along behind him. Sorry. Sorry. And my head nods. Up and down. Yes, sir. How clever, sir. Fancy us not realising that, sir. What an immensely clever and gifted man you are.

The trouble is, of course, he is. Immensely clever. Immensely gifted.

In theatre . . . I forget . . . I watch him. He has ginger hairs on the backs of his hands . . . he holds his hands out for the gloves . . . tufty ginger hairs, dry skin, and biscuit coloured freckles. And those repulsive, stubby little hands . . . the delicacy, the skill . . . You should see him . . . he takes the knife . . . he skims away the wafer of donor skin . . . he places it . . . a smooth and pale surface masking the raw wound, the angry tissue, the pain . . .

'For God's sake, Dr Kovacs, stop crowding me.'

I'm so fascinated, though. That's the trouble. I forget. The artistry of it . . . the reconstruction of surfaces.

Sometimes he passes the Watson knife to me. 'Go on, go on. You do it.' But his presence there paralyses me. I can feel his criticism burning through my neck. He becomes irritated. He loses all patience. 'No, not like that! Good God.' The difficulty is, you see, having drifted into this by mistake, no, not by mistake, more by an inability to make the right decisions . . . or, indeed, any decisions at all . . . I've now found the one thing that fascinates me, the one thing that I choose to do. Donald Preston has got a job at one of the London Teaching Hospitals. This means there's a vacant registrar's post. I made a decision. I chose. I put in an application. I won't get it, of course. I know that. But still.

And she goes into EFFIE'*s room.*

Good morning.

EFFIE *turns away.*

(*A little awkwardly:*) You're still . . . Look, I'm sorry if I upset you yesterday.

EFFIE: I remember him saying it. Effing brat. 'E did say that. All the time.

Pause.

I could've made the other up, though. I don't remember.

DR KOVACS: You've been touching your head. That's how infections start. Let's see your arms. Any swelling?

EFFIE: No.

DR KOVACS: Let me see.

A pause while she works.

And what about the matches?

EFFIE: What matches?

DR KOVACS: Did you make that up too?

EFFIE: I didn't have no matches.

DR KOVACS: That's what I mean. Is that a story as well?

EFFIE: Matches was against the rules. So I couldn't of had none, could I? No matches, no food in your room. No visitors after eleven. No smoking.

DR KOVACS: At Crampton Court?

EFFIE (*this amuses her*): Crampton Court! No, Miss. The Laurels. This house they took us. They come into Somerville one day, they say, 'Oh Effie, see, ent that nice, you're going to have your own room in your own house and you can do whatever you like in it'.

DR KOVACS: Fires don't just start for no reason.

EFFIE: No scissors. No alcohol. No putting your bed where you want it.

DR KOVACS (*bringing her back to the subject*): Effie.

EFFIE: They can do.

DR KOVACS: Not in the middle of beds, Effie. The fire started in your bed.

EFFIE: You been checking up on me.

DR KOVACS: We have notes about all our patients.

EFFIE: Well, it did. I said that. I always said it started in the bed, didn't I? It's them what says I'm lying. Whoosh.

DR KOVACS: So you must have had matches or a lighter or something.

EFFIE: Whoosh. Burn your house down.

DR KOVACS: Mustn't you?

EFFIE: 'It'll be ever so nice there, Effie,' they says. 'At The Laurels. Free to do whatever you fancy. Go to the pictures. Have your hair done.'

(*Happy memory:*) We had the pictures every Saturday night at Crampton Court, Miss. Every Saturday. In the dining-room. Fridays we had a dance. Sundays they come and sung for us. Choirs and that. We had little girls come doing their dancing once. They was ever so pretty, Miss.

(*Demonstrating:*) Hey little hen, when when when will you lay me an egg for my tea? Tap tap shuffle tap shuffle tap shuffle tap.

She comes over slightly embarrassed.

Pause.

And Mondays we had library. Tuesday the lady come to do our hair. And the beauty lady if you wanted your nails and that done. Thursday was the day the lady come to do our feet. We was ever so busy, Miss.

The burst of enthusiasm fades.

They said, 'You'll have a lovely room at The Laurels all your own, Effie.'

DR KOVACS: You didn't like it?

A pause.

EFFIE: I had a cupboard once.

DR KOVACS: Pardon?

EFFIE: A cupboard . . .

DR KOVACS: For keeping your clothes in?

EFFIE: Don't think I had no clothes.

DR KOVACS: You must have had clothes. What was in the cupboard then?

EFFIE: Things. Boots. A gun. Some old rags. Odd bits of things.

DR KOVACS: On the farm?

EFFIE: And I used to sit there all by myself. (*Singing*:) Lavender's blue, dilly, dilly, Lavender's green, When you are king dilly dilly I will be queen . . .
Knock knock. Who's there? Noah. Noah who? Noah, can't come in, ever, cos tis my room in yere. Mine.

DR KOVACS: Why a cupboard?

EFFIE: Lavender's green, dilly dilly, I will be queen . . .

DR KOVACS (*making her answer*): Effie!

EFFIE: Knock knock. Who's there?

DR KOVACS (*slightly exasperated*): I am, for goodness sake.

EFFIE *stares at her for a moment and then bursts out laughing.*

EFFIE: That's not funny, Miss.

DR KOVACS: Then why are you laughing?

EFFIE: It's supposed to be a joke, Miss. You spoiled it.

DR KOVACS: No, you spoiled it. *I'm* supposed to say 'Who's there?'

EFFIE: No rules, Miss. Not in jokes.

DR KOVACS: There are, Effie.

EFFIE: Always worked with Alice. We used to have good laughs me and Alice. Things she said.

And this reminds her.

Where's Alice gone?

DR KOVACS *has glanced briefly at her watch. Now the time registers. She is thrown into disorganised panic.*

DR KOVACS: Oh Lord, no! That can't be right. I'll have to go, Effie. I'll come and see you tomorrow. All right?

EFFIE: Yes, Miss.

DR KOVACS *dashes out, tearing off gloves.*

DR KOVACS: Due in theatre twenty minutes ago.
In trouble again. Blah, blah, blah. As if I were fourteen. A lecture on my responsibility to the other patients. A lecture on my responsibility to the team.
'Yes, Mr Jessop Brown. I'm sorry. I'm so sorry. I got held up.'
'Fundamental rule, Dr Kovacs. We do not get involved with our patients' problems. Leave it to the medical social workers.'
I know. I know . . .

(*Calming down slightly*:) In the afternoon I rang Crampton Court. Alice who? they said.
I'm afraid I don't know. Just Alice.
'Well, we've got several Alice's here,' they said.
Alice who was a very good friend of Effie Palmer's?
'Oh, Alice Whittingham, you mean? Transferred to The Laurels. One of our rehabilitation hostels.'
I used the phone in Sister's office.
'Ah,' he said. Poking his head round the door. 'Dr Kovacs. Sister not in? Never mind. Wanted a quick word with you anyway.' And I was caught completely off guard. He said he'd been thinking very seriously about things. He said he had of course carefully considered my application for the registrarship . . . he'd noted my

interest in theatre . . . nevertheless, fundamentally . . . and he started calling me Ruth . . . 'fundamentally, Ruth . . . and this is in no way a criticism of your work . . .'

(*Her thought*:) Isn't it?

'No,' he said, 'the fact of the matter is, Ruth, my dear, that fundamentally, and indeed temperamentally, I feel you're not entirely suited to this sort of unit. A lot of women find that, you know.' So avuncular. So kind suddenly. No jokes. Not one. 'In the end, Ruth,' he said, 'they find they're really much happier, much more effective, working in General Practice.'

I don't want to go into General Practice. I don't want that. I'm going to be a surgeon.

That's what I should have said. Straight out. To his face. I should have said 'Mr Jessop Brown . . .' . . . But I didn't. I didn't say anything. I was completely . . .

'Well,' he said, 'you think about it, my dear. Give it careful thought.'

She goes into EFFIE's *room.*

EFFIE *looks up, alarmed.*

EFFIE: What's the matter, Miss?

DR KOVACS: Nothing.

EFFIE: You look sick, Miss.

DR KOVACS: Let's have a look at that infected arm. Hold it still.

EFFIE: I am holding it still. Tis you, Miss.

DR KOVACS *starts undoing the dressing on the infected arm. Her hands are shaking with repressed anger.*

(*Mumbling to herself*:) Bad, dirty Effie.

DR KOVACS: Hold it still.

EFFIE: Bad inside. Festering.

DR KOVACS: Rubbish. It isn't festering at all. It's drying up. Healing very nicely.

EFFIE *examines her arm.*

EFFIE: They said I was.

DR KOVACS: Who did?

EFFIE: Bad, dirty Effie. I was sitting in my cupboard when they come for me.

DR KOVACS: When who came for you? I don't know what you mean, Effie.

EFFIE: In a van. Come screeching up the lane into the yard. And my dad says: 'She's in there. In there. You get her.' And they pull open the door and they drag me out. I was kicking. Screaming. I bit one of 'em. And then they pushed me into the van and they sat on me.

DR KOVACS: Who did? Who were they?

EFFIE: They tied my hands up like that.

She lets her arms dangle helplessly in front of her like the long sleeves of a strait-jacket.

DR KOVACS: Like that? You mean round here?

She folds her arms round her body to demonstrate.

EFFIE: Yes.

DR KOVACS (*beginning to work it out*): And they took you to Crampton Court?

EFFIE: In a van. And my mum . . . my mum she stood there in the yard with a face like stone. Like stone. Watching.

DR KOVACS: Your mother . . .?

EFFIE: Like stone.

DR KOVACS (*appalled*): How old were you, Effie?

EFFIE: Twelve. Thirteen. Don't want to waste no pretty name on that effing brat.

DR KOVACS: They took a thirteen-year-old away in a strait-jacket?

EFFIE: Cos I was kickin' 'em, see.

DR KOVACS: That's no reason. I'd've kicked them too. I think.

EFFIE: And they give me an injection, Miss. And me and Alice, we wasn't on Somerville Ward then. We was downstairs on the unmanageable ward. She was unmanageable too. My dad, see, Miss, he went to the council and they had me on a section.

DR KOVACS: What on earth had you done?

EFFIE: I don't know, Miss. Don't remember. Bad dirty dreams. (*She lifts her hands up to her head.*)

DR KOVACS: Don't touch it. (*The burn wound on her head.*)

EFFIE: I don't want to talk about it, Miss.

DR KOVACS: We'll leave this dressing off, then. If it starts to itch don't scratch. Effie, I said if it itches, don't scratch. (*Going.*) I'll get the nurse to come and put some cream on later. Help you sleep.

EFFIE (*mumbling*): Don't want to sleep. Bad dreams.

DR KOVACS *leaves the room.*

DR KOVACS: Straight to the phone. 'Crampton Court? Yes, I did. I did ring you earlier. About Alice Whittingham. I now need some information about my patient Effie Palmer.'

And they said: Very sorry, but they couldn't go into details because the relevant records had been lost during the war.

But that was over forty years ago. Why wasn't she released?

And they said: 'But Dr Kovacs, she was released. She was moved to The Laurels last summer.' They said it was now government policy to move as many long-stay patients as possible into the community.

But why was she there in the first place?

And they said: Well, as far as they knew she'd been categorised under section 1 part D of the 1927 amendment . . .

What does that mean?

It means, they said, that she was classed as a moral defective.

What on earth is a moral defective? A not very bright little girl of thirteen classed morally defective? On whose terms?

She goes into EFFIE's *room.*

Good morning. Sleep well?

EFFIE: No.

DR KOVACS: No, nor did I.

EFFIE: Bad dreams. Keep remembering things. Police come again.

DR KOVACS: Did they? What did they say?

EFFIE: There's going to be a hearing, Miss. About the fire.

DR KOVACS (*about* EFFIE's *face which she is examining*): That looks all right.

EFFIE: No, it don't. Seen it in a mirror, Miss.

DR KOVACS: It'll look better when it's healed. By the way, I rang up Crampton Court yesterday. I asked them about your friend Alice.

EFFIE (*suddenly alert*): Alice? Where's she gone to?

DR KOVACS: They said she'd been transferred to The Laurels.

EFFIE *thinks hard.*

So you were both transferred to The Laurels? She was with you?

EFFIE (*after some more thought*): Stupid name. Weren't no Laurels. Weren't no nothing. Little spitty bit of a garden. They said 'Effie, we're going to close Somerville Ward.' I said 'Close it? You can't close it.' I didn't know what they meant.

A pause. Then a slow smile.

I chose the curtains, Miss. Yellow ones. They said 'Effie, we're going to have new curtains on Somerville. What colour would you like?' And I said – yellow.

It was safe there. We had the tele. I knew everybody. All the staff. Everybody. 'Hello, Effie.' 'Morning, Eff. You all right today, Eff?'

Me and Alice we had such good times. You could walk in the gardens if you wanted. You could sit there if it was warm. Watch everything.

'How can you close it?' I said.

'It's all right, Effie. It's going to be all right. You're going to have a room all your own . . .'

I got my own room. This is my room. My bed. Alice's bed. Dot's bed. Yellow curtains.

DR KOVACS: Careful with your arm.

EFFIE: They wanted it, Miss. Not me. I would of chose to stay, but no, we all had to go whether we wanted to or not. And they kept saying: 'Ent you lucky? Ent you a lucky girl, Eff?' And then this van come just like we was going to Weston for the day and we all had to get in. And me and Alice, we sat like this. (*Demonstrating their degree of apprehensive tension.*) 'Going to take you to see your new house, Effie. You'll like that.' 'No, I won't.' 'Yes, you will. Do what you want now.' Course, 't'was a lie. 'Cos what I wanted to do was go back home. To Somerville. But I couldn't do that, could I?

You don't know where she's gone then, Miss?

DR KOVACS: I don't know where she is now. I'll do some more investigating for you, if you want.

EFFIE: And you tell that policeman I didn't have no matches.

DR KOVACS (*carefully*): Effie, when they came for you in the van . . .?

EFFIE: Me and Alice, Miss, we sat like this.

DR KOVACS: No, not that time. The first time. When you were in the cupboard.

EFFIE: And my mum watching. Face like stone.

DR KOVACS: That time. Why did they come? What had you done.

EFFIE (*confused pain*): I don't know, Miss. (*A pause.*) See . . . (*Then changing her mind.*) No, no, I can't. Could've been a dream. I don't know.

DR KOVACS *says nothing, but waits.*

I can't.

A pause.

See, one time I was crawling in the hedges cos I was looking where this hen we had was laying. She was off by herself, see, in the hedges. So this man . . . he come down the lane . . . he saw me and what he done he pushed me through t'other side into Longacre and he done it to me.

A long pause.

DR KOVACS: Did you know the man?

EFFIE: No. I seen him before but I didn't know his name.

DR KOVACS: Did you tell anyone?

EFFIE: No.

DR KOVACS: How old were you?

EFFIE: Don't know. Eleven. Twelve. Didn't know what he was going to do at first. Thought he was going to kill me, see, when he was so rough pushing me through the hedge. Every time he saw me he done it. Then there was another one, he started. He worked over Potter's Farm, t'other side of the wood.

DR KOVACS: Didn't anybody tell you it was wrong, what they were doing?

EFFIE: My mum and dad done it.

DR KOVACS: Yes, but . . .

EFFIE: I seem em doing it.

DR KOVACS: I suppose so.

EFFIE: Didn't think about it. T'was just how it was. And that feller from Potter's Farm, he give me sweeties. He give me a ribbon once. 'Where'd you get that,' my dad said? 'Found it,' I said. In the wood.

DR KOVACS: So you did know it was wrong?

EFFIE: Don't know. Say 'Where'd you get that?'

DR KOVACS: Where did you get that?

EFFIE: No. No. In a bad voice.

EFFIE (*in a voice of authority that startles both of them*): Where did you get that?

EFFIE (*automatic response*): Found it.

Pause.

See. Frightened me. So I told a lie. Found it.

A pause.

So then I starts to get fat. Like that. And my dad says, ''Cos she eats too much'. And my mum thinks: No, it ent, and she took me down her sister's and she says: 'Is it what I think, Cissie?' And they dug their fingers in. Like that. And she says, 'Yes, tis'. And my mum says, 'Oh God, ow'm I going to tell him, Ciss?' And she says, 'Effie, who done that to you?' And my aunty says, ''Tis no good. She don't know what you mean. She'm too daft.' My mum says, 'Effie, have any men come along and took your drawers off and done them sort of things to you?' And I says 'Yes'. And my aunty she says 'Win, you'll have to do summat with her'.

And then we goes home and my mum's crying and saying 'Oh God, ow'm I going to tell him?' And my dad . . . my dad says 'Effing brat. Underneath the field hedges with any old dirty bugger that comes sniffin' round. Got a name now for it, ent she? Any bugger wants it, go'n find Effie Palmer. She'll give it yer.'

And then after that . . . (*She frowns in a muddled, vague way as if uncertain quite what did happen after that.*) . . . after that they comes for me in the van. My dad says I was out of control. He said he was going to beat I. 'Bloody flay her alive,' he said. So I shut myself up in my cupboard and I held on to the door when anyone come. My dad said, 'Leave her, Win. She'll come out when she'm hungry'. But I wouldn't come out, see. I wouldn't. And they come and they pulled open the door and I screamed and I kicked and they pushed me into the van and they sat on me. I couldn't breathe, Miss.

And my mum's face was like stone. Watching.

A long pause.

DR KOVACS: What happened to the baby?

EFFIE: What?

DR KOVACS: The baby?

EFFIE: What baby?

DR KOVACS: Your baby.

EFFIE (*vaguely*): I don't know. Don't remember.

DR KOVACS: You don't remember the baby being born?

EFFIE (*after some thought*): Yes. Remember that. Remember the pain. (*More thought.*) T'was a little girl.

DR KOVACS: What happened to her, Effie?

EFFIE: Dunno.

DR KOVACS: Did you ask?

EFFIE: 'Can't have a baby living here, Effie, can we? Crampton Court's no proper place for a baby, is it? We'll find a nice home for her.'
Don't remember.

DR KOVACS: Oh, Effie . . .

EFFIE: I'm tired now, Miss.

They are both lost in thought. Then DR KOVACS *makes a move.*

Will you come tomorrow, Miss?

DR KOVACS: Yes.

EFFIE (*surprised*): You crying, Miss?

DR KOVACS: No. Just . . .

As she comes out, helplessly, to the audience:

Just . . .

She struggles hard not to cry. Some hair is falling down. She pins it up.

Just . . .
And there he was. He and his team. At the end of the corridor.
'Ah! What an honour. What a privilege. Behold. Dr Kovacs . . . more or less . . . with the exception of a hair pin or two . . . looking a little disarranged today, Dr Kovacs. Not, I hope, allowing our emotions to get the better of us?'
'No, Mr Jessop Brown. Everything under strict control.'
(*Still slightly amazed at herself:*) Yes and that's what I said. I actually said it. To his face.
Do you know, I think if I were not under strict control all the time . . . all the time . . . if I once let one half of what's in here out, then the ceilings would crack, the floors would open, the roofs fly off slate by slate into the air, girders buckle, pavements open up, forests rip apart and swirl into the clouds, the seas boil, the skies grow black . . .

She gathers herself back under control.

As it is, however, I keep the surfaces smooth and cover up the pain. It's the only way. The only way.

And she moves towards EFFIE's *room.* EFFIE *looks up.*

EFFIE: You've been crying.

DR KOVACS (*blowing her nose*): No, I haven't. I've got a lot on my mind. I don't know what to do.

EFFIE: You do what you want, Miss. Don't let them tell you stories. 'Ent this nice? Aren't you a lucky girl then, Eff?'

DR KOVACS *manages to pull herself together. After a moment*:

Is it dinner time yet?

DR KOVACS (*amused despite herself*): Soon. Why? Are you hungry.

EFFIE: They said: 'When you go the Laurels, Eff, you'll be able to have your dinner whenever you wants.' And Alice says: 'So what?' she says. 'Crampton Court we always do have our dinner whenever we wants to have our dinner 'cos whenever we wants to have our dinner it's always dinner time, innit?'

DR KOVACS (*amused*): And when you were ready for bed it was always bed time. Is that right?

EFFIE: Yes, Miss.

DR KOVACS: It's called institutionalisation, Effie.

EFFIE: Yes.
'Well,' they said, 'this is the kitchen, Effie. This is where you can make your dinners. This is Mrs Williams . . . she'll come in, give you a hand. Help with the shopping and that.'
I didn't like it.
And they said 'This is your room, Effie'. I couldn't sleep in there. Never slept on my own. Never. The dark come pushing in through the window. I couldn't find where I was in there. I couldn't sleep. 'S'all right, Eff, love,' Alice said. 'I know what us'll do.' And what we did, we pushed my bed into her room. But Mrs Williams and the social workers, they said 'No, dear, you can't do that. That's against the rules.'
And Alice said . . . 'You told us we could do whatever we want now, so we did, didn't we, Eff? This is what we want.'
And they said: 'Yes, but moving beds about is against the rules, innit?

You live in a community now, you got to have rules. You had rules at Crampton Court, didn't you?'
And Alice said: 'Well, we didn't have to move the beds at Crampton Court did we? We was all right there.'

And they are both laughing.

She always come out with a good answer, Alice.

A pause.

So they put Alice in a room downstairs.

(*Suddenly, in a bleak, lost voice*): Knock knock. Who's there? No one.

DR KOVACS: It's all right, Effie.

EFFIE (*not hearing, lost in her memory; the panic*): Nobody. She wasn't there. Not in the kitchen, not in the lounge. Not in her room . . . the bathroom . . . the toilet. Where's Alice gone to?
'Alice was a disruptive influence, and done you no good. We think you'll both settle down a lot better if you're apart for a while. So what we've done, we've moved Alice to another house.'
I says: 'What house? You can't go moving people round just cos it suits you.'
Tell you what they didn't like, Miss. They didn't like it when Alice and me had a good laugh together.
You find her, Miss. You find her and then we'll go home.

DR KOVACS *hurries out.*

DR KOVACS: All morning on the phone to the Local Authority. I learned a lot. Alice Whittingham. Committed under Section 2 aged fourteen. Moral defective. Her father, an insurance clerk and her mother, a housewife, could neither of them, in their cramped pre-war suburban gentility, cope with the social disgrace of having a daughter they'd discovered to be six months pregnant let alone with the stigma of having a daughter who was a bit lacking.
'But where is she now,' I said.
'Well, she was moved from Crampton Court when the long stay wards were closed . . .'
Yes, I know that. To The Laurels.
'That's right. To The Laurels. Profoundly unco-operative, it says

here. Subsequently moved to Heatherwood.

Where's that?

'On the other side of town. Near the by-pass. Another of our halfway houses. Oh dear. Cerebral embolism, it says here – October 28th. Did you know about that? Died November 1st.

Alice Whittingham is dead?

'That's right.'

As a result of being mucked about once too often.

'No, as a result of a massive stroke, Dr Kovacs. She was 67. I don't think there's any need to be abusive.'

No, no, of course not. I'm sorry. Sorry.

There I am apologising again.

(*Suddenly very angry:*) Yes, there's every bloody need to be abusive. Every bloody need. Two little girls who weren't very bright and who offended . . . innocently offended . . . against what I think are called prevailing social mores, were put away, behind locked doors, nice and tidy, and forgotten because they were an embarrassment to public respectability. And the years passed and they grew to be two old ladies who'd made a life for themselves. In a quiet ordered place. All right . . . all right, it was a lunatic asylum. It was an ugly piece of Victorian institutional architecture, but they walked in the garden, they had their films, they chose their curtains. And meantime society changes. Meantime society says: Dear me, what a shocking thing we did. And what a lot of money we're wasting. Let's kill two birds with one stone . . . Hah! Two birds with one stone. That's good. I'll tell Effie that one. There's a joke for you . . . let's give those two old ladies their freedom. And save a lot of money while we're at it. But the old ladies are frightened. They don't know what to do with it. A useless gift. Freedom to them is the safe space they've always known surrounded by ordered gardens, not a tiny room surrounded by infinite chaos. People should be very careful when they bandy words like freedom about.

She becomes embarrassed by her outburst. It fizzles away.

She starts a slow handclap.

'Oh well, done, Dr Kovacs. Well done. Never heard you so eloquent. Well done.'

She stares for a moment. Then turns towards EFFIE*'s room.*

'And where are you going now?' he said. 'You do realise that you're due in theatre in ten minutes?'

She turns back, uncertain. Then:

I'm sorry. I've got something very important to do first.

'You are assisting me in theatre, Dr Kovacs. We start at precisely two o'clock. In nine minutes' time.'

DR KOVACS *hovers uncertainly for a moment. Then she makes her choice. She turns and goes to* EFFIE*'s room.*

At the door, she pauses and gathers herself:

How am I going to tell her?

EFFIE (*distressed*): I thought you wasn't coming.

DR KOVACS: I got held up. I've been on the phone.

EFFIE: The police come again.

DR KOVACS: It'll be all right, Effie.

EFFIE: What you saying that for? You don't know that.

DR KOVACS: No. I'm sorry. But I think . . .

EFFIE: There's going to be a hearing. What will they do, Miss? Where will I go?

DR KOVACS *sits down.*

DR KOVACS: Effie . . . I found out about Alice for you.

A pause.

EFFIE (*struggling to remember things*): Alice is dead, ent she?

DR KOVACS: Yes.

EFFIE: It come through. Suddenly. I remembered.

DR KOVACS: It was a stroke.

EFFIE: They come and told me. I was thinking all last night . . . Where did they send her? And then I remembered.

I was in my room. They says 'Come on, Effie, why don't you go for a nice walk down the shops? Why don't you come downstairs and watch the tele?'

(*Stubbornly repeating what she's said over and over again*:) Where's Alice gone?

And they says, 'You move all that furniture away from the door and come out of there, and we'll explain all about Alice.'

You tell me now and then I'll come out.

And they said, 'Alice isn't with us any more.' They said what a blessing it was really.

And I sat on my bed. And everything in here boiled up and boiled up . . . (*Holding the sheet she starts to stand.*)

'You going to say something, Effie?' they said.

I didn't know what to say, So much . . . boiling up . . . I thought if I opened my mouth to say it . . . if I let it out . . . so I sat there with my mouth closed and I wouldn't say nothing to them.

'All right, Effie,' they said. 'You want to be left alone, we'll leave you alone.'

(*She is standing now, a defensive, terrified figure holding the sheet*): And the darkness pressed in through the windows. And I could hear the boiling getting louder and louder and I was afraid that if I . . .

She presses the sheet to her mouth.

DR KOVACS: What? – Then what?

And the pent-up anger explodes. She suddenly flings the sheet away and stands there full of power like a column of flame.

EFFIE: And then it poured out of my mouth, out of my arms . . . great walls of it . . . streaking up them silly curtains . . . dancing all round the room . . . and I burned their house down, Miss, I burned their house down.

DR KOVACS: Oh yes, Effie. You did. You did.

EFFIE: I did. I burned it down. And I can do it again.

The moment passes.

They'll have to send me back to Crampton Court now, won't they? (*No response.*) Won't they?

DR KOVACS: I don't know, Effie. I don't know what they'll do.

EFFIE: Will you speak for me, Miss?

DR KOVACS (*alarmed*): Me?

EFFIE: Will you? At the hearing? Will you tell them? It'll be all right then.

DR KOVACS: Not necessarily.

EFFIE: You got the words. You can explain.

DR KOVACS: I can't explain that, Effie. They'll say: Dr Kovacs, you're a rational human being, a scientist. You know perfectly well how fires start.

EFFIE: Yes, and you'll say, it don't matter whether she had matches or not, do it? That's got nothing to do with it. That's not the point. And then you'll tell them. Will you, Miss?

Slight pause and then:

DR KOVACS: I'll try.

She turns away.

I said: 'Mr Jessop Brown, I'm taking Wednesday off. I'm giving evidence in Court.'

And he opened his mouth to say something; something exquisitely painful, another small pinprick . . . too small to complain about without sounding absurdly petty . . . but when added to all the other small pin-pricks . . .

But before he had time to shape it, before he had time to dip it in poison, I said: Don't bother. It's not a request. And I may as well tell you, Mr Jessop Brown, that I am not withdrawing my application for the registrarship. I know I won't get it, but I'm not withdrawing it, and I'm not going into General Practice either simply to suit you, to suit your prejudices. I'm staying here. And while I'm on the subject, I suggest you find someone else to laugh at now, because I'm getting very bored with it. And no one actually finds it funny.

Then:

No, of course I didn't. I didn't say that at all. But something like it. Something very like it. (*She smiles.*) And he knew what I meant.

Effie's Burning

Effie's Burning was written for the now defunct Lunchtime Season at the Library Theatre, Manchester. It was an excellent season, which every year allowed four or five new writers the chance of a real professional production, and for this reason if for no other it's greatly missed. Workshops and rehearsed readings are fine but they can't teach a writer new to theatre half as much as can a two-week rehearsal period followed by a two-week run.

As far as I was concerned, it allowed me the chance to write for a medium which had always terrified me. The theatre seemed to me a particularly male stronghold. I suppose subconsciously I'd made a rather crude division between novelists and radio playwrights who were pre-eminently women, and television and theatre writers who were pre-eminently men. I felt that to write for the theatre would be to trespass in a closed, slightly hostile environment, and to wrestle with a medium I didn't really understand. I'm not sure, even now, why I accepted the commission: probably because John Durnin, the assistant director who was in charge of the lunchtime season, and Dave Simpson, resident writer, assured me that everything would be all right; and anyway, at the time of commissioning it all seemed so far away as to be almost academic.

Certain restrictions were placed on these lunchtime plays: for obvious reasons they couldn't last longer than an hour, the set had to be small enough to fit inside a pre-existing set, and simple enough to be set up and struck every day, and the cast had to be kept to a minimum. This ruled out any possibility of armies massing on battle-scarred, Brechtian wastes, or chanting choruses, or any of the ingredients I had somehow assumed necessary to theatre. In the event, however, pressure of work meant that there was no time to worry about their loss. *Effie's Burning* had to be written at enormous speed more or less at the same time as I was writing for a television series, so that I turned up finally at rehearsals feeling exhausted, defensive and quite unprepared for what I was certain was going to be an alarming and unpleasant experience.

Contrary to all expectations, it was one of the happiest and most fruitful experiences of my life. Susan Sutton Mayo, the director, had already earned my respect when, in the face of my incoherent ramblings, she explained what the play was about. 'Well,' she said, 'I think it's a play about power', which was like inserting a sharp crochet hook into my head and pulling all the frayed and tangled threads into a clear pattern, probably the single most useful thing a director can do for a writer. She and I, the cast – Paula Tilbrook who played Effie and Brigit Forsyth who played Dr Kovacs – and our stage manager, met every day for a fortnight either in a rehearsal room or more frequently in the social club at Ringway airport; and between us we created what seemed at the time, and still seems in retrospect, a very special working atmosphere. There was a freedom to be completely open and relaxed with one another and to offer a kind of safety which made criticism constructive and liberating. It was an enormous privilege to watch what happened to the script when the creative powers of such a director and such a cast was brought to bear on it; and at the end of the rehearsal period there was a degree of trust and support between us which seemed to make anything possible.

So this is dedicated particularly to Sue, Paula and Brigit who later braved many horrors for the sake of the play, and to whom *Effie's Burning* really belongs.

Valerie Windsor trained as an actress. She has written ten radio plays including *Variation on a Snow Queen* which won the Pye/Society of Authors Award for the Best Radio Play of 1981, and *Myths and Legacies* which won a Giles Cooper Award in 1987. Both plays were directed by Kay Patrick. Valerie Windsor has also written for television, including working for a year on *Brookside*. A new television play is currently in production. *Effie's Burning*, which was nominated for a Manchester Evening News Theatre Award, was her first play for the theatre; but two further plays are scheduled for 1988.